Using Student Tracking Systems Effectively

Trudy H. Bers, *Editor*
Oakton College

NEW DIRECTIONS FOR COMMUNITY COLLEGES
ARTHUR M. COHEN, *Editor-in-Chief*
FLORENCE B. BRAWER, *Associate Editor*

Number 66, Summer 1989

Paperback sourcebooks in
The Jossey-Bass Higher Education Series

Jossey-Bass Inc., Publishers
San Francisco • London

EDUCATIONAL RESOURCES INFORMATION CENTER

Clearinghouse For Junior Colleges

UNIVERSITY OF CALIFORNIA, LOS ANGELES

Trudy H. Bers (ed.).
Using Student Tracking Systems Effectively.
New Directions for Community Colleges, no. 66.
Volume XVII, number 2.
San Francisco: Jossey-Bass, 1989.

New Directions for Community Colleges
Arthur M. Cohen, *Editor-in-Chief;* Florence B. Brawer, *Associate Editor*

New Directions for Community Colleges is published quarterly
by Jossey-Bass Inc., Publishers (publication number USPS 121-710),
in association with the ERIC Clearinghouse for Junior Colleges.
New Directions is numbered sequentially—please order extra copies
by sequential number. The volume and issue numbers above are
included for the convenience of libraries. Second-class postage paid
at San Francisco, California, and at additional mailing offices.
POSTMASTER: Send address changes to Jossey-Bass, Inc., Publishers,
350 Sansome Street, San Francisco, California 94104.

The material in this publication is based on work sponsored wholly
or in part by the Office of Educational Research and Improvement,
U.S. Department of Education, under contract number RI-88-062002.
Its contents do not necessarily reflect the views of the Department,
or any other agency of the U.S. Government.

Editorial correspondence should be sent to the Editor-in-Chief, Arthur
M. Cohen, at the ERIC Clearinghouse for Junior Colleges, University
of California, Los Angeles, California 90024.

Library of Congress Catalog Card Number LC 85-644753

International Standard Serial Number ISSN 0194-3081

International Standard Book Number ISBN 1-55542-863-0

Cover art by WILLI BAUM

Manufactured in the United States of America. Printed on acid-free paper.

Ordering Information

The paperback sourcebooks listed below are published quarterly and can be ordered either by subscription or single copy.

Subscriptions cost $60.00 per year for institutions, agencies, and libraries. Individuals can subscribe at the special rate of $45.00 per year *if payment is by personal check.* (Note that the full rate of $60.00 applies if payment is by institutional check, even if the subscription is designated for an individual.) Standing orders are accepted.

Single copies are available at $14.95 when payment accompanies order. (California, New Jersey, New York, and Washington, D.C., residents please include appropriate sales tax.) For billed orders, cost per copy is $14.95 plus postage and handling.

Substantial discounts are offered to organizations and individuals wishing to purchase bulk quantities of Jossey-Bass sourcebooks. Please inquire.

Please note that these prices are for the calendar year 1989 and are subject to change without notice. Also, some titles may be out of print and therefore not available for sale.

To ensure correct and prompt delivery, all orders must give either the *name of an individual* or an *official purchase order number.* Please submit your order as follows:

Subscriptions: specify series and year subscription is to begin.
Single Copies: specify sourcebook code (such as, CC1) and first two words of title.

Mail orders for United States and Possessions, Latin America, Canada, Japan, Australia, and New Zealand to:
Jossey-Bass Inc., Publishers
350 Sansome Street
San Francisco, California 94104

Mail orders for all other parts of the world to:
Jossey-Bass Limited
28 Banner Street
London EC1Y 8QE

New Directions for Community Colleges Series
Arthur M. Cohen, *Editor-in-Chief*
Florence B. Brawer, *Associate Editor*

Contents

Editor's Notes

In spite of many challenges, institutions are implementing student tracking systems that are working. The chapters in this volume describe some of these and discuss some more general concerns and issues related to tracking the flow of community college students through higher education.

In Chapter One Trudy H. Bers presents a conceptual model of student flow through an institution, which is a valuable background for any discussion of student tracking systems. She briefly outlines the purposes of student tracking systems and comments on the tension between the theory and the practice of designing and implementing tracking systems.

In Chapter Two Ann Kieffer Bragg establishes the context within which many tracking systems are being initiated, designed, and implemented: state mandates, including legislation, policies, rules, and practices. The variety among states is astonishing, as is the rapidity of changes in this domain.

Chapters Three through Eight focus on tracking system segments that exemplify the stages in the student flow model presented in Chapter One. The inquiry stage is represented by Alison Rutter Barrett's description in Chapter Three of a preadmissions tracking system used at a small, rural community college. Determined to keep the system as personal as possible, the staff relied first on a manual, paper process. Over a three-year period, however, they moved to the use of a computer, while continuing to personalize communications as much as possible.

Richard A. Voorhees and Sharon Hart in Chapter Four discuss tracking as it relates to the entry stage of the student flow model. They focus on a tracking scheme for basic skills intake assessment, and the efficacy and logistics of linking data from assessment with other, longitudinal data to permit long-term tracking of students.

Several chapters relate to the experience stage of community college student flow. In Chapter Five Pat Smittle, Michael R. LaVallee, Jr., and William E. Carman describe a tracking system for underprepared students. Located in Florida, their college has had to respond to a number of state mandates for monitoring students. In Chapter Six Melvin L. Gay and Costas S. Boukouvalas describe a system for tracking and monitoring students in special groups, such as learning disabled and hearing impaired. Finally, in Chapter Seven Trudy H. Bers and Alan M. Rubin present examples of the difficulty of relying on computer programs to identify and communicate with students in academic difficulty while still making room for human intervention and professional judgment. In doing so, they illustrate some of the limits of computer tracking systems in serving students' needs.

Chapter Eight by Michael R. Stevenson, R. Dan Walleri, and Saundra M. Japely relates to the follow-up stage of the student flow model. It discusses the role of follow-up studies in tracking student progress, and in particular argues the importance of including data about students' intentions in compilations of student data and for the analysis of follow-up studies.

The final three chapters of this volume explore tracking from a view broader than the institutional perspective. In Chapter Nine Stanley I. Adelman, Peter T. Ewell, and John R. Grable describe LONESTAR, a longitudinal tracking system developed for a consortium of Texas community colleges by NCHEMS. Prompted by a new state mandate related to remedial education, LONESTAR is designed both to respond to short-term reporting requirements and to facilitate long-term tracking of students.

In Chapter Ten Judith W. Leslie presents a novel description of the place of computers in tracking systems. Using the analogy of the theater, she describes various "plays," or activities, in which students engage, such as assessment and registration, and the "role" of the computer in each.

Finally, in Chapter Eleven, Jim Palmer provides an overview of the trends and issues in student tracking systems.

Trudy H. Bers
Editor

Trudy H. Bers is senior director of institutional research, curriculum, and strategic planning at Oakton College, Des Plaines, Illinois.

This chapter defines the various factors that currently emphasize the need for comprehensive student tracking systems in community colleges.

Tracking Systems and Student Flow

Trudy H. Bers

Several factors have recently joined to promote significant interest in tracking students as they progress through higher education and beyond. The first factor is marketing. In particular, colleges' concerns about attracting and retaining students are prompting many activities: identifying and maintaining communications with students who inquire about an institution, identifying and working with students experiencing academic or social difficulties to increase the possibility that they will remain at the institution, and enhancing efforts to stay in touch with alumni to generate donations and to build positive public relations.

The second factor is accountability, or outcomes measurements. Constituents of higher education—legislators, state governing boards, governors, trustees, employers, and parents—are demanding evidence that the programs they fund are producing the expected results. While it is hard to argue with the legitimacy of their request in general terms, conflicting definitions of *success,* difficulties of measuring complex learning, and logistical nightmares of data collection and analysis make these requests burdensome if not impossible.

The third factor prompting renewed effort to track students is an internal emphasis on teaching and learning. Part of teaching and learning is finding out whether students do indeed achieve the levels of affec-

T. H. Bers (ed.). *Using Student Tracking Systems Effectively.*
New Directions for Community Colleges, no. 66. San Francisco: Jossey-Bass, Summer 1989.

4

tive, behavioral, and cognitive growth the college expects them to as a result of their educational experience.

A fourth factor is the need to communicate with the growing diversity of community college students in an efficient, effective manner. A tracking system can provide students with accurate information in a timely and accessible manner about their status at the institution, as well as about such issues as level of academic skills, transferability of courses, progress toward a degree, and services available.

And finally, internal competition for scarce resources is placing severe pressure on many programs and services to demonstrate their effectiveness. It is no accident that many initial efforts to track students focus on remedial programs, programs that frequently are considered to be expensive yet tangential to the core mission of colleges and universities. Required to "prove" their worth, remedial program staff and faculty have begun to design sophisticated tracking programs to monitor students' progress. Once operative, these tracking systems foster spin-off questions about how students came to the institution in the first place, and how they do when enrolled in college-level courses and after they leave the college.

In summary, tracking systems can respond to needs for information at many levels: the student, the college (including individual departments), and the state. While the specific types of data required by each level vary, a comprehensive system can be designed to accommodate all needs. Actually doing so is, however, no easy task, yet it is a task that is commanding increasing attention from educators everywhere.

Conceptualizing Student Flow Through a Community College

Before developing a comprehensive tracking system, it is useful to distinguish various stages through which a student moves at a college. Then one can identify research and data collection methodologies, data storage and retrieval requirements, and reports needed to monitor student flow among these stages. Student flow through a community college can be conceptualized as comprised of six stages. Though presented here as if they occurred in linear sequence, in fact community college students may move back and forth among the stages once the first one has been completed.

1. *Awareness Stage.* Prospective students first become aware of the college. They may have diffuse or inaccurate perceptions, and they obtain their information from a variety of sources. From the college's point of view, the major factor differentiating this stage from subsequent ones is that during this stage prospective students are not identifiable as individuals, nor is there any way to contact them except through mass mailings

to households or businesses, the media, public information sessions, or other generalized formats for contacting the public.

2. *Inquiry Stage.* Prospective students make contact with the institution, either through their own initiative or in response to college outreach efforts. In either case, prospective students are now identifiable by name or social security number, may have noted a particular area of interest or major, and may even begin to supply the institution with such data and information as an application form, high school and college transcripts, and test scores. Individuals may also seek very specific information about programs or counseling/advisement sessions.

3. *Entry Stage.* Prospective students formally apply, are admitted to, and enroll in the institution. They take assessment tests if these are required or recommended, and they may participate in orientation, advisement, and registration sessions. It is only after formal registration occurs and classes have begun that any yield figures (enrolled students divided by admitted students) can be calculated.

Since community colleges are open-enrollment institutions that require little if any advance application or acceptance for most programs, the stages of application and acceptance—very discrete stages in the recruitment process of many senior institutions—are merged into one in the model presented here.

4. *Experience Stage.* Students are taking courses at the college. It is at this stage that most tracking efforts have been directed, in order to monitor academic progress, offer support services such as tutoring, and engage in retention activities.

5. *Completion Stage.* This is actually the final component of students' experience at the college. Students either complete a degree, certificate, or desired courses, and therefore presumably meet their objectives, or they exit the college without completing these educational goals. Sometimes, though rarely, exit is imposed by the institution if students fail to meet the college's academic (or other) standards. However, most often exit is voluntary, and in the case of community colleges occurs prior to the students' earning a degree or certificate.

6. *Follow-Up Stage.* Students are considered alumni and, at the same time, given the character of community colleges, can also be considered prospective students. Various follow-up studies may be conducted to obtain evaluations of programs and services, identify possible new courses or programs to attract former students back to the institution, and assess the employment and academic histories of students subsequent to their exiting the community college.

Tracking Is Easier Said Than Done

Tracking students through higher education is a difficult task, especially in community colleges. Monitoring the progress of students and drawing general conclusions is a challenging task at best, due to characteristics of both the community colleges and the students who attend them:

- Many community colleges are only now developing application and admissions procedures that will enable them to collect and maintain data about students beyond the minimum demographic and transcript data necessary to award grades and degrees
- The sporadic, mostly part-time attendance patterns of community college students, making it difficult to discern when students have actually exited the college
- The large number of years that students may attend the college—five or more years is not unusual
- The attendance by students at multiple institutions through the course of their collegiate studies (in some colleges students who transfer from senior institutions back to the community college are nearly as numerous as those who enroll at the community college as first-time college students)
- The vast majority of students—as many as 90 to 95 percent in some colleges—exit the institution "for good" prior to earning a degree or certificate
- The incomplete or nonexistent sharing of information among colleges and universities about the progress and performance of individual students.

Challenge of Tracking

Tracking and monitoring the performance of community college students is a challenging endeavor. It is easy to become focused on the technical aspects of computer-based systems, the production of sophisticated reports, and even the preparation of multicolor graphic representations of data. The real challenge, however, rests in ensuring that whatever tracking and monitoring systems are implemented in an institution or a state, they support the teaching and learning that are the core mission of community colleges. Consequently, divergent pressures must be reconciled.

There may be perceived contradictions between relying on computer technology to handle large amounts of data and communications and the proven effectiveness of personal contacts linking a student with the college. There may appear to be contradictions between amassing aggregate data about groups of students through standardized tests and providing meaningful feedback to individual students about how they are doing. There may be a tendency to saturate students with testing, registration, advising, tracking, and evaluation information beyond that which they can absorb and use. And there may be conflicts about the extent to which colleges will share information with each other about students who transfer.

Tracking students through postsecondary education is clearly receiving attention and resources. It will probably be at least another half decade before fully integrated systems are in place, tested, and refined. Only then will educators be in a position to assess whether the projected benefits warrant the obvious costs.

Trudy H. Bers is senior director of institutional research, curriculum, and strategic planning at Oakton College, Des Plaines, Illinois.

State initiatives for improving the collegiate experience point out the need for colleges to develop student tracking systems.

Beyond the College: State Policy Impact on Student Tracking Systems

Ann Kieffer Bragg

Current interest in educational reform grew out of the turbulent economic conditions of the past decade. Unprecedented inflation followed by recession and an increasingly negative trade balance eroded confidence in the nation's economic competitiveness. Education was touted as both the cause of and the solution to the nation's economic ills.

The *A Nation at Risk* report, issued by the National Commission on Excellence in Education in spring 1983, described the nation's public education system as "eroded by a rising tide of mediocrity" (p. 11). That report recommended increases in requirements for high school graduation and college admissions. It also recommended the use of standardized achievement tests at what it called "schooling transition points" (p. 15).

The companion piece on higher education, *Involvement in Learning* (Study Group on the Conditions of Excellence in American Higher Education, 1984), was issued in spring 1984. While acknowledging that higher education was not in as dire straits as elementary and secondary education, this report recommended the strengthening of the general education portion of the baccalaureate degree and supplementing "the

T. H. Bers (ed.). *Using Student Tracking Systems Effectively.*
New Directions for Community Colleges, no. 66. San Francisco: Jossey-Bass, Summer 1989.

credit system with proficiency assessments both in liberal education and in the student's major as a condition of awarding degrees" (p. 46).

While other reports provided impetus to faculty members and administrators to undertake curricular reform, *A Nation at Risk* and *Involvement in Learning* prompted state-level initiatives for enhancing the quality of undergraduate education.

Calls for assessment of student outcomes and attention to general education were picked up by the National Governors' Association in its report *Time for Results* issued in 1986. The governors adopted six recommendations for improving quality and requested state action on each by 1991. Among the recommendations were the implementation of comprehensive assessments of student learning and the provision of incentives to improve undergraduate education.

The National Governors' Association report was followed in 1987 by the State Higher Education Executive Officers' (SHEEO) policy statement on program and institutional assessment, which asked states to develop uniform definitions of retention and graduation rates. It also requested institutions to assess students' achievement of general education objectives and to use alumni satisfaction, student performance on licensing and certification exams, and successful transfer or employment in judging the quality of individual programs.

The remainder of this chapter will review trends in state responses to these calls for reform and the diversity and similarity among states in quality improvement initiatives. Then, it will discuss implications of these quality initiatives for the development of community college student tracking systems.

Trends in State Responses

Historically, states were involved primarily in two aspects of higher education: the chartering of new institutions and the allocation of public funds. Beginning in the 1960s, however, one state after another created a superboard either to govern or to coordinate the state's higher education enterprise. A first task of these superboards was to develop a state master plan for higher education to delineate the mission of each type of institution and the specific role of individual institutions. An early example of these master plans was the California Master Plan, which only now is being reexamined. Another task of most superboards was to rationalize the state's higher education budget request and allocation process.

In addition, at the time of their establishment, the superboards in twenty-three states were authorized to approve new programs requested by at least one sector of higher education in the state. This program approval authority was later added in other states, so that by 1983 the boards in forty-seven states had the authority to approve new programs.

At the same time, many boards were given authority to review existing programs. While in 1960 only a few boards had program review authority, by 1983 the boards in forty-three states had program review authority for at least one sector of higher education (Barak, 1984). The authority to review existing programs marked the states' transition from primarily fiscal to educational performance concerns.

Already questioning the scope of remediation in higher education— for example, California, Illinois, Maryland, Minnesota, and Texas, among others, completed remediation studies—and prompted by *A Nation at Risk,* states turned their attention to remediation's natural partners: admissions requirements and basic skills testing of entering students. The Southern Regional Education Board (SREB) noted this interrelationship in 1985 when it recommended the adoption of statewide course placement standards, statewide basic skills testing, and remediation programs for all of its members. New Jersey, the front-runner in mandating a statewide basic skills assessment at college entry in 1977, was followed by Florida, Georgia, and Tennessee. Arkansas and Texas will begin administering statewide basic skills tests in fall 1989 (National Governors' Association, 1988b).

The Virginia Council on Higher Education recommended admissions requirements in 1983, the University of North Carolina system adopted new requirements effective for fall 1990, the Illinois Board of Higher Education adopted course-specific admissions requirements for all public institutions effective in fall 1990 (a date delayed to fall 1993 by the legislature), and the South Dakota state legislature adopted similar requirements in 1985. The proposed California community college matriculation model, although similar in intent, so far mandates neither statewide admissions requirements nor a statewide basic skills test. From 1983 to 1985, about one-quarter of the states strengthened admissions requirements (Newman, 1987).

Admissions requirements, basic skills testing, and remedial programs as efforts to improve the quality of higher education concentrate on the input rather than the outcomes side of the ledger. Beyond these entry-control efforts, the SREB (1985) recommended statewide junior-rising exams (exams that end-of-year sophomores must pass to enter the junior year), such as were already in place in Florida and Georgia. Texas plans to implement a junior-rising exam in 1989–90, and Oklahoma is considering one (National Governors' Association, 1988b). Six states—Connecticut, Kansas, Maryland, Nebraska, Tennessee, and Virginia—have considered but rejected this concept (Jaschik, 1987). Other states are opting for value-added assessment measures to improve programs. For example, New Jersey is field-testing a statewide General Intellectual Skills test, as part of its College Outcomes Evaluation Program (*Report to the New Jersey Board . . . ,* 1987).

Rather than adopting statewide programs, the majority of states, through the state board's planning, program review, or budgeting authority, are requesting institutions to implement their own comprehensive assessment programs (Boyer, Ewell, Finney, and Mingle, 1987). For the most part, these efforts are just getting under way.

Diversity and Commonality Among States

Diversity. Because state higher education systems differ in size, complexity, and organizational structure, their responses to calls for reform differ in origin, sector participation, institutional involvement in decision making, and reporting mechanisms. In some states, initiative came from the state legislature. For example, the California Assembly Concurrent Resolution 141 (1986) directed the California Postsecondary Education Commission, with the assistance of a task force, "to . . . make recommendations relative to talent development, value-added, and performance-based budgeting approaches to measuring and improving the quality of education" (California Postsecondary Education Commission, 1987, p. 16). The Minnesota legislature formed the Task Force on Quality Assessment in Postsecondary Education in 1987 to "determine the goals of quality assessment [and] to study and select strategies and mechanisms the State can use in achieving these goals" (National Governors' Association, 1988b). In Michigan, the legislature required only community colleges to submit annual degree information as a measure of outcomes (Illinois Board of Higher Education, 1987).

In other states, the governor was more instrumental. For example, in Missouri, the Council on Public Higher Education made a commitment to the governor in 1986 to establish assessment programs on all member campuses. Wisconsin's effort, begun as a pilot project by the University Board of Regents, was expanded and formalized by the governor but then was not funded by the legislature (Illinois Board of Higher Education, 1987).

In still other states, quality initiatives evolved as part of the higher education board's regular responsibilities. For example, after several years of experience in program review, the Illinois Board of Higher Education in September 1986 adopted recommendations by its Committee on the Study of Undergraduate Education that require institutions to "assess individual student progress in meeting the objectives of general education and the development of baccalaureate-level skills" (p. 48) as part of the program review process and require the state to establish a system to monitor student performance statewide.

Rhode Island also incorporated assessment into its program review process, while in New Hampshire and New York learning outcomes information was incorporated into the planning process.

In most states, new quality improvement initiatives, whether by legislative or board action, apply to all public institutions as is seen, for example, in Illinois, Maryland, New Jersey, Rhode Island, Tennessee, and Utah. Alabama, however, began its process with four-year institutions, while Michigan's legislation applied only to community colleges. Both Alabama and Georgia are reviewing the role and mission of two-year institutions only (National Governors' Association, 1987b).

In some states, widely representative groups determined the need and established guidelines for implementing assessment programs and other quality improvements, such as the Illinois Committee on the Study of Undergraduate Education, the Kansas Council of Chief Academic Officers, and the Missouri Council on Public Higher Education. In other states, representative committees were formed to develop plans and guidelines for implementing programs whose need and sometimes basic form were already determined, such as the California Task Force, the New Jersey Advisory Committee for the College Outcomes Evaluation Program, and the Outcomes Committee of Michigan community colleges. In still other states, such as Alabama and Rhode Island, guidelines developed by the board's staff were presented for comment before adoption.

Reporting mechanisms also differ among states. In some—for example, Alabama, Arizona, and Colorado—institutions must submit assessment plans to the board for review in one year, with annual results reports beginning a year later. In others—for example, Connecticut, Illinois, and Maryland—only annual reports of assessment results are to be submitted. Other states—such as New Jersey, Ohio, and Rhode Island— have offered competitive incentive grants to institutions to establish assessment programs. Two states have built financial incentives into their budgeting process. Tennessee's performance-based funding program, implemented in 1979, provides institutions a bonus of up to 5 percent for various quality improvements. Beginning in 1990, the Colorado Commission on Higher Education "can withhold up to two percent of an institution's appropriation if the institution has not implemented" a value-added assessment program (National Governors' Association, 1987, p. 34).

Commonality. Despite these differences among states in style and structure, the similarity in actions is unmistakable. The National Governors' Association (1987) first annual follow-up report showed that within the last five years, twenty-six states more clearly defined the role and mission of each institution, twenty-two states were developing comprehensive assessments of undergraduate student learning, and nine states provided institutions with financial incentives to improve undergraduate education. The second annual report (National Governors' Association, 1988a) shows that only fourteen states have not implemented and are not currently considering implementing some form of outcomes assessment.

Whether assessment is initiated by the state or by an individual institution, there are seven features common to assessment programs being established across the country.

First, the ultimate goal of assessment programs is to improve teaching and learning. To be effective in improving teaching and learning, faculty members, both full- and part-time, must be actively involved in both the design and implementation of the assessment process. The assessment process must also build in appropriate mechanisms for communicating the results of assessment to individual students to guide their educational decisions and mechanisms for incorporating aggregated assessment results into institutional decision making in order to take action to improve programs.

Second, the assessment programs being developed or already implemented measure student learning over time. Using a longitudinal or value-added approach, most programs measure student learning at entry, at the end of the sophomore or beginning of the junior year, at the end of the senior year, and after graduation.

Third, most assessment processes measure student achievement of both general education skills and knowledge objectives and knowledge in the major. While program review has occurred in many institutions and has been mandated by many states for years, recently initiated assessment programs are including this new general education dimension.

Fourth, the assessment programs developed so far use multiple measures of student learning. Commercial or locally developed tests are used to measure basic skills at college entry for admission or course placement, at mid-career to measure knowledge of general education or general intellectual skills, and at graduation to measure knowledge in the major field of study. Surveys, commercial inventories, and interviews of students and alumni are used to measure changes in attitudes and values, involvement in learning and in the institution, and satisfaction with the program of study and the institution. Alumni follow-up surveys at short- and longer-term intervals are used to provide information on success in employment or further education. Finally, common statistics such as retention, graduation, and job placement or transfer success rates are derived and compared over time for student cohorts and for specific programs.

Fifth, most assessment programs assess not only individual student progress but also aggregate data on individual progress in order to determine strengths and weaknesses and, then, to take action to improve programs and services. Although individual students are tested and surveyed, results are generally aggregated to identify program strengths and weaknesses as the basis for program improvement, instead of using the results to promote or bar the promotion of individual students.

Sixth, a reporting procedure is established. Within the institution, close working relationships are required between individual departments and college deans and between departments or colleges and central administration in the collection and analysis of information at the most appropriate level and in the preparation of comparative reports. Reports also are needed for external constituents. For example, Oregon provides freshman progress information to high schools, and North Carolina and Texas report statewide community college to university transfer success information. Information also is given to the students, such as placement test results, progress in remediation, and results from junior-rising, general education, or major exams.

Finally, most states involved in assessment require institutions to submit assessment reports either annually as part of the mission review, planning, or budgeting process or cyclically as part of program review. In many states, such reports are submitted in a specified format, while in states with computerized student unit record systems, data may be transmitted in machine language. Since many states are just beginning the process—in some states, for example, assessment plans are to be submitted between 1987 and 1989, while others are requiring the first annual implementation reports in 1988 to 1991—reporting formats have yet to be determined. While the expressed purpose of state-mandated assessment programs is program and institutional improvement, one consequence of such programs is likely to be the comparison of like programs among institutions and the use of assessment data to document how well individual institutions are fulfilling their roles and missions.

Implications for Community Colleges

Student Tracking System Design. A comprehensive community college assessment program must be multipurpose in design if it is to be useful. The assessment program should be designed to meet not only any state requirements but also the needs of the college's already existing planning, program review, and budgeting processes and the self-study requirements of regional accrediting agencies. If an assessment program is to be worth the time, energy, and cost of development, it must produce information useful in making decisions about program improvement and the future of the college.

Since assessment programs are in the early stages of development in most states, community college faculty and administrators need to become involved at the state level in establishing program guidelines, deriving common data-element definitions, and developing reporting formats. What constitutes a program, for example? Which students should be tracked and for how long—degree seekers only or course takers as well? How should college-preparatory students, such as students enrolled in adult basic or secondary education or English as a second language programs offered by community colleges, be handled? At the very least, community colleges need to be able to track students according to their enrollment intent, so that students who intentionally enrolled in only one or two courses are not classified by the state and compared with university data as degree dropouts.

A comprehensive assessment program requires a system to monitor or track individual student progress. Such a student tracking system needs to be carefully planned with input from users such as departmental faculty both before any data are collected and after an inventory is developed to determine what information is already regularly collected, how and in what form it is collected, and how and by whom it is analyzed and used.

For efficiency, the college's student tracking system needs to be computerized. The system, for example, should be able to extract or download data elements already available on other college record systems, such as admissions, registration, transcripts, and graduation audits, in order to avoid duplicate collection and entry efforts. It should be easily modifiable and expandable in order to accommodate new data elements determined necessary either by a later evaluation of the process or by external mandates. At the same time, definitions of data elements need to remain consistent over time to permit longitudinal analysis. Accuracy in coding and in data entry, of course, must be assured. The student tracking system needs to be constructed to allow for the drawing of random samples or cohorts for special analyses and to protect the privacy of individual students. Finally, the data collection procedures need to be routinized and incorporated into the ongoing processes of the college so that the definitions and the need for the information are taken as a matter of course. Endo and Bittner (1985) and Ewell (1987) present excellent technical discussions of building computerized student tracking system files.

Design Problems and Pitfalls. A chief reason for designing the student tracking and other computerized information systems prior to any attempt to gather data is that such systems are costly to develop and maintain both in personnel time and in computing costs due to the number of students and number of data elements in the data base. Which students and which data elements to include should depend on the objectives the assessment program is meant to achieve. Thus, in the construction of the data base, each element should serve a specific purpose, and informational elements without specific purposes should be excluded. In the design stage, the college also needs to examine the trade-offs between the complexity and comprehensiveness necessary to answer the basic design questions and the ease of use of the system. Who will have access to the computerized data? Is extensive training necessary, and if so, who will receive it, who pays for it, and what will be the effects of turnover?

Designing an assessment process and the student tracking and other systems needed to support it must take into account the methods of analysis and interpretation, as well as what data are to be collected. Raw data in reams of computer printouts or tables of numbers are not information. Data must be synthesized, analyzed, interpreted, and cogently presented to be usable to the different decision makers involved—faculty, administrators, and state agencies. Thus, in designing the process, reporting formats and time lines also need to be developed. Kinnick (1985) gives examples of formats designed for different audiences. In establishing time lines, compromises may be necessary between completeness and timeliness. For example, if planning for the succeeding year begins in the spring, only fall rather than annual data may be available, while if planning for the succeeding year begins in the fall, annual data may be available.

Finally, to avoid misinterpretation of information, periodic interaction is needed between those responsible for the data collection and interpretation and the end users. While such interaction within the college may be relatively easy, time must be set aside for this purpose. Interaction between the college and the state agency, however, is also necessary and may not be as easy. Since the state agency or board is likely to produce synoptic reports that permit comparison among institutions within and among states, it is imperative that colleges assure the accuracy of the information submitted and the board's interpretation of it. Many state boards already have formal or informal advisory committees, while others circulate drafts of reports for review and comment. Other boards may be willing to do so if asked. Concerned college representatives need to serve on such committees or groups and to follow up on solicitations of advice.

Conclusions

Historical trends indicate that state monitoring of higher education will continue for the foreseeable future. Additional states are likely to adopt the policies recommended by the National Governors' Association and other groups. Community colleges in states that have not mandated assessment programs would do well to initiate such programs on their own. While the costs of mounting assessment programs and the student tracking and other computerized data systems needed to support them may be high, a comprehensive assessment program may be the best means of providing the college the information needed to continue to improve the quality of the teaching and learning process and to attest publicly to the achievements of its graduates.

References

Barak, R. J. *State Level Academic Program Review and Approval: 1984 Update.* Denver, Colo.: State Higher Education Executive Officers, March 1984.

Boyer, C. M., Ewell, P. T., Finney, J. E., and Mingle, J. R. "Assessment and Out-

18

comes Measurement: A View from the States." *AAHE Bulletin*, 1987, *39* (7), 8-12.

California Postsecondary Education Commission. *Funding Excellence in California Higher Education: A Report in Response to Assembly Concurrent Resolution 141 (1986)*. Sacramento: California Postsecondary Education Commission, March 1987.

Endo, J., and Bittner, T. "Developing and Using a Longitudinal Outcomes Data File: The University of Colorado Experience." In P. T. Ewell (ed.), *Assessing Educational Outcomes*. New Directions for Institutional Research, no. 47. San Francisco: Jossey-Bass, 1985.

Ewell, P. T. "Principles of Longitudinal Enrollment Analysis: Conducting Retention and Student Flow Studies." In J. A. Muffo and G. W. McLaughlin (eds.), *A Primer on Institutional Research*. Tallahassee, Fla.: Association for Institutional Research, 1987.

Illinois Board of Higher Education. *Report of the Committee on the Study of Undergraduate Education*. Springfield: Illinois Board of Higher Education, September 1986.

Illinois Board of Higher Education. Letter to State Higher Education Executive Officers, Fall 1987.

Jaschik, S. "Most State Officials Shun Uniform Tests as a Way to Measure Progress of Students." *Chronicle of Higher Education*, February 25, 1987, pp. 28, 29.

Kinnick, M. "Increasing the Use of Student Outcomes Information." In P. T. Ewell (ed.), *Assessing Educational Outcomes*. New Directions for Institutional Research, no. 47. San Francisco: Jossey-Bass, 1985.

National Commission on Excellence in Education. *A Nation at Risk: The Imperative for Educational Reform*. Reprint. *Chronicle of Higher Education*, May 4, 1983, pp. 11-16.

National Governors' Association. *Time for Results: The Governors' 1991 Report on Education*. Washington, D.C.: National Governors' Association, 1986.

National Governors' Association. *Results in Education: 1987*. Washington, D.C.: National Governors' Association, 1987.

National Governors' Association. *Results in Education: 1988*. Washington, D.C.: National Governors' Association, 1988a.

National Governors' Association. *Results in Education: State-Level College Assessment Initiatives—1987-1988, Results of a Fifty-State Survey*. Washington, D.C.: National Governors' Association, 1988b.

Newman, F. *Choosing Quality: Reducing Conflict Between the State and the University*. Draft manuscript. Denver, Colo.: Education Commission of the States, 1987.

Report to the New Jersey Board of Higher Education from the Advisory Committee to the College Outcomes Evaluation Program. Trenton: Office of College Outcomes, New Jersey Department of Higher Education, 1987.

Southern Regional Education Board. *Access to Quality Undergraduate Education: Text of SREB Panel's Report*. Reprint. *Chronicle of Higher Education*, July 3, 1985, pp. 9-12.

State Higher Education Executive Officers. *A Statement of Policy by the State Higher Education Executive Officers on Program and Institutional Assessment*. Denver, Colo.: State Higher Education Executive Officers, 1987.

Study Group on the Conditions of Excellence in American Higher Education. *Involvement in Learning: Realizing the Potential of American Higher Education*. Washington, D.C.: National Institute of Education, 1984.

Ann Kieffer Bragg, formerly the director of program planning for the Illinois Community College Board, is currently completing student assessment and minority student achievement projects for the Illinois Board of Higher Education.

The enhancement of communication with prospective students can strengthen college marketing efforts.

Keeping Your Admissions Office on Track: A Community College Perspective

Alison Rutter Barrett

College admissions offices continue to become increasingly sophisticated in their methods of recruiting students. Purchased names from national testing agencies, innovative promotional activities, personalized letters, and flashy publications are used to contact and generate inquiries from prospective students, who may then be invited to participate in a host of academic programs, activities, and services.

Maintaining contact with prospective students from the point at which they become known to the institution, at least through the time they enroll or decide not to enroll, is considered crucial to effective recruitment processes. This chapter focuses on the approach used by Cochise College in Douglas, Arizona, to track and maintain contact with prospective students. It also examines the relative advantages and disadvantages of relying on computer software packages or staff members to manage the tracking process.

T. H. Bers (ed.). *Using Student Tracking Systems Effectively.*
New Directions for Community Colleges, no. 66. San Francisco: Jossey-Bass, Summer 1989.

Admissions Tracking

Admissions tracking is the process of following prospective students from the time they inquire about the college through the admissions cycle. It consists of an in-house management system that enables the college to stay in touch with prospective students as they move through the admissions process. While tracking does not itself recruit students, the enhancement of communication with prospective students can strengthen college marketing efforts.

Admissions offices store information about prospective students in a variety of ways, ranging from jammed folders in file cabinets or bent index cards to sophisticated data base management programs on personal or mainframe computers. It is often difficult for institutions to determine the data elements they will need to collect and store to track students, and to develop a system to file, store, and retrieve information effectively. My uncle says he has a very simple filing system—whenever he needs certain information, he just goes through all of his information. Perhaps that works for dresser drawers, but admissions offices must look toward more practical solutions to prospective student tracking problems. As each college is different, so each college must determine its own requirements for prospective student data.

The colleges and universities that have honed the tracking of prospective students to a fine art for the longest time are those institutions that are residential, selective, independent, and whose students are young, full-time, and relatively homogeneous. Such schools maintain contact with prospective students throughout the junior and senior years of high school with tailored letters and telephone calls, anticipating that a certain percentage will apply, be accepted, and enroll in the fall semester following high school graduation. Much of what is written about tracking systems is based on the experience of such schools, who rely on their systems to help them predict the size of the incoming freshman class and to diversify their student bodies by attracting students with differing characteristics (for example, academic ability, race, geography).

Community College Concerns

Community colleges face special difficulties in developing and implementing admissions tracking systems. The greatest difficulty stems largely from the diverse backgrounds of students who choose to attend a community college, or who at least express interest in attending. Community college students do not fit into a small number of easily defined categories, as Helfgot (1986) observes: "Community college student characteristics are notable by their range . . . —the lowest and the highest social strata . . . , those fitted with intellectual superiority . . . , those of every ethnic and social subculture . . . —for formal and informal educational experiences. . . . Community college students often attend part-time and whenever their other life activities permit a few hours to direct to education. Their attendance is sporadic and is almost always woven into a life consisting of many other interests and obligations" (p. 22). The admissions office at Cochise College realized very quickly that trying to force information about community college students into a tracking system designed for traditional students would never bring successful results, and we set about designing and implementing a system that would work for our institution.

The Great Paper Chase

Cochise College is a public community college located in a rural setting in southeastern Arizona. There are 4,500 students from a variety of backgrounds who attend classes at two campuses and several community locations throughout the county. Until three years ago Cochise College had no inquiry tracking system. Requests for college information were simply answered, and no precise records were kept. We recognized that we were missing out on an opportunity to reach, at a later time, those who expressed interest in the college and to provide information pertinent to them as individuals. Our purpose in developing our tracking system was twofold: to provide a more personal approach to working with prospective students and to evaluate our recruitment efforts. This was quite different from simply using the number of names in the data base to predict the size of the incoming freshman class, yet our purpose was well suited to the community college philosophy and to our prospective students.

Our first rudimentary attempt relied on paper. Each time a prospective student had contact with the admissions office, whether it was through a campus visit, letter, telephone call, transcript, ACT or SAT score sheet, or an information request form completed during a college visit to the high school, all the information we could determine about that student was listed on a paper "prospect form." Data elements were name, address, phone number, area of academic interest, high school, and the way in which the prospective student learned about Cochise College. The admissions office then sent the requested information and recorded the college response on the prospect form. The forms were filed in alphabetical order in a file cabinet.

The system was cheap. It was also next to useless. Only the most general information could be tracked effectively. The greatest fault was that we tracked only traditionally aged students because their data were the most accessible. Thus in developing our first tracking system, based on traditional student models, we failed to include the largest group of students attending Cochise College: the adult returning to school.

The nontraditional or adult student is difficult to identify. Often the admissions office is unaware of these prospective students' interest in the college before they appear with an application for admission in one hand and a registration form in the other. We knew that we would need to look toward a more creative system to include nontraditional students.

Out of the File Cabinet and into the Computer

Our first step toward a more functional tracking system was to purchase a personal computer (an IBM-compatible model with a twenty-megabyte hard disk) and to investigate software options. While software developed specifically for an individual admissions office can address the unique needs of that office, custom programming is much more expensive than commercial packages, and the admissions office staff must be very clear about their expectations of the software. At the same time, it is important to clarify information needs prior to investing in commercial software in order to assure that the purchased program will meet office requirements.

Due to budget limitations and the need to put a system into operation quickly, we selected a commercial admissions software program called HelperOne produced by the College Board. This program has worked well for our tracking needs. It has many user-friendly aspects, and instructions are easy to follow. In fact, we were entering prospective student data the day the program arrived.

Keeping Track of It All

Once the software was installed and we learned to use it, we embarked upon the next step in developing a useful admissions tracking system. We focused on learning as much as possible about our prospective students so we would have a complete record in the computer for future use. To accomplish this we divided our prospective students into two main groups—traditional and nontraditional. We categorized as traditional all high school students and anyone under the age of twenty-one. Nontraditional referred to prospective students aged twenty-one and older. A separate code exists for each group. ACT and SAT score sheets, transcripts, return mail requests for information cards, and most letters provide enough information to determine the category in which to place prospective students.

Students whose inquiries are made by telephone are more difficult to categorize, and so we designed a telephone request form. Now when callers request information we ask for their names, addresses, the semester in which they plan to enroll, and how they learned about Cochise College. We then ask if they would like to be added to our mailing list. If they say yes, we ask about their areas of interest or educational goal and the length of time they have been out of high school. The prospective students' responses provide the admissions office with enough information to categorize them as traditional or nontraditional students.

As mentioned previously, adult prospective students can be an elusive lot. Their needs for information about college opportunities are as diverse as they are. It is often difficult even to identify them to enter them into the tracking process, and it is equally as hard to know how much of which kind of information they require in making a decision about attending college. Word of mouth seemed to be the most common way that adults were learning about Cochise College. In order to increase the general public's knowledge about the college throughout the county, we focused our efforts on an awareness campaign, utilizing billboards, letters to the parents of high school students, advertising inserts in local newspapers, mailings to area employers, and talks with service clubs and organizations. Each activity gave prospective students a means of contacting the college for more information, which encouraged a response and at the same time gave us a means of evaluating the campaign. We surveyed our community prior to the campaign and found that a majority of county residents did not know much about the college. While we have yet to survey the community following the campaign, the increase in the number of requests for information from adults has shown that a far greater number of nontraditional students have expressed an interest in Cochise College than before. The campaign encouraged them to contact the admissions office early, and thus we have been able to enter information into our data base and include inquirers in prospective student mailings.

The major difference between the information sent to nontraditional students and traditional students is that traditional students receive more mailings that include less information, while nontraditional students receive fewer mailings containing more detailed information. The reason for this difference is that we receive the majority of names of traditional prospective students during the fall semester prior to their enrollment the following fall semester; consequently, we have a much longer period of time in which to correspond with them. Nontraditional students, on the other hand, generally contact us only a month or two prior to enrolling— thus they need as much information as possible in a shorter period of time.

When the admissions office receives a request for information and we are unable to determine the traditional or nontraditional status, we answer the request but do not enter the scant information into the computer. Only information that could be useful at a later time is stored. This keeps our computerized files from becoming cluttered with irrelevant data.

Currently our data base is small—about 2,000 records. We anticipate the number will double next year. We expect eventually to maintain a data base of approximately 5,000 records, although the hard disk would enable us to more than double that number.

We review prospective student data on the computer data base on a monthly basis, and names are deleted when we determine a lack of continued interest. High school student records are kept in the system until the fall after students are scheduled to graduate. If the admissions staff has been corresponding with a student for a year, however, and he or she has not responded at all, we consider dropping the name from our records. Generally nontraditional prospective students are maintained in the system for a year from the time of their first inquiry. After that time, the admissions staff reviews the record and determines whether or not to retain the name. HelperOne allows us to record the dates that prospective students contact the admissions office and the dates that we correspond with them so we can quickly review a printout of students' records and judge the level of interest over a period of time. If mail is returned to our office as undeliverable, we drop the record immediately. While we must review the records ourselves, the HelperOne program does have a purge function so that all records marked for deletion may be removed at one time. While there is certainly an advantage to a program that automatically purges files that show no activity for a stipulated time period, we appreciate that our manual system is flexible and have been thankful more than once that a name was not deleted automatically.

Benefits and Drawbacks of the Tracking System

We have found several important benefits resulting from our prospective student tracking system. The involvement of college faculty and staff in providing information for the computer tracking system has been a special bonus. Understanding that prospective students have contact with the college in a variety of ways, we in the admissions office believed that the first contact with many students did not occur through the admissions office. Indeed, we believed that many students had virtually no personal contact with the admissions office, ever. Consequently, we asked college departments that have contact with prospective students to send any information about them to our office so we could serve as a central location for maintaining information. We now regularly receive information from instructors, the financial aid and housing offices, and from a large number of college staff.

The admissions office asked each department for cooperation through a series of meetings on marketing. We worked closely with the departments to show that we were not trying to take away their ability to correspond with prospective students but rather wanted to enhance their efforts. While forms were made available to department chairs to use to forward prospective student information to the admissions office, the majority of departments informally write names and addresses on notebook paper and memo pads, or send actual letters that prospective students have written to them. The format does not matter—the fact is that we are now getting more information. While a few department chairs have chosen not to cooperate, the majority view a central office as a benefit in corresponding with prospective students; it saves the department chairs time and they know that prospective students are receiving good service and personalized information. This cooperation between college departments has enhanced communication and has given faculty and staff a sense of involvement with the college's marketing efforts.

A second benefit, which can also be a disadvantage, is that our tracking system allows us operate independently from other college offices, such as the computer center. We have the capability to run mailing labels or generate letters without relying on others; however, an independent data base is not as accessible to other individuals or departments as a centralized data base is and may also lack professional staff support.

A third benefit is that the tracking system enables us to evaluate the effectiveness of certain recruitment and promotion techniques. For example, Cochise College recently rented billboard space to advertise one of our academic programs. Since we now have information on how prospective students learn of and make contact with the college, we were able to determine the number of prospective students who saw the billboard and then subsequently enrolled. We had data enabling us to demonstrate that billboard advertising in that particular location was a worthwhile promotional activity.

The greatest benefit has been in the response of students to our personalized mailings. I recently asked a student from England why he had chosen to attend Cochise College. His response was that the admissions office had provided him with the information he needed about the program he wanted to enter, had answered all of his questions, and was the first college to respond to his request for information. When we began our tracking system, we did not know what to expect, but again and again people tell me how much they appreciate being treated as individuals, not numbers.

The biggest drawback to our current system is duplication of effort. Since our inquiry tracking system is not a part of the college's mainframe computer system, we must manually enter all information about a prospective student into the mainframe system as soon as we receive an application for admission, even though much of that information already resides on the tracking system data base. While we are investigating a tracking system that would be integrated with our mainframe system, so far we have chosen to keep the personal computer system because of its flexibility, data storage capability, and independence from other computers.

Keeping Contact Personal

Computers have the capability to store practically unlimited amounts of information, but they have gained the bad reputation of making communication impersonal. The warning "do not fold, spindle, or mutilate" generally refers to paper and computers, but it also refers to prospective students, especially in community colleges, which attract many for whom college is a first and frightening experience.

We wanted to use our tracking system to generate letters to prospective students expeditiously, and so we knew we would be using a computer printer for letters. We did not, however, want to risk alienation by sending generic, computer-printed letters. We were given an option some time ago to purchase a dot matrix printer, which would have allowed us to more than double the number of letters printed each hour. We chose to keep our slower, letter-quality printer, so that each letter would appear typewritten and would have a more personal look.

We use college letterhead paper for our prospective student letters, and they are all written with a conversational and informal tone. Our initial letters are brief, with sufficient space left at the end of each letter for the admissions staff to add handwritten comments. We have separate letters for traditional and nontraditional prospective students, based on type of inquiry (a letter, telephone call, or campus visit) and residence (in county or out of county). Our inquiry letter bank contains twelve versions of an initial contact letter. We also maintain a listing of paragraphs that are answers to the questions asked most frequently. We insert these paragraphs into the body of our letter; the paragraph begins, "To answer your question about . . . " We currently do not answer questions about specific academic department offerings, but we do have on file answers to fifty questions concerning the admissions process, financial aid, housing, placement testing, and athletics. Whenever we answer new questions asked by prospective students, we add the answers to our letter bank.

The tracking system provides us with a means to learn as much as possible about prospective students, so that information sent to them is as personal as possible and targets their special needs and interests. With our system we have been able to develop a calendar for contacting prospective students several times throughout the inquiry phase, thus capitalizing on the fact that people remember information better if it is received over a period of time, instead of all at once. While the schedule in Figure 1 is not comprehensive, it is a sampling of the amount of information sent to prospective students, regardless of whether they apply

**Figure 1. Schedule of Mailings to Prospective Students
(Cochise College, Douglas, Arizona)**

Date	Traditional Prospective Student	Nontraditional Prospective Student
Within twenty-four hours after contact	Four-color folder describing Cochise College, with information on admissions, financial aid, housing, placement testing, and activities; an application for admission; and:	
	Personalized letter focusing on options beyond high school and responding to questions	Personalized letter focusing on job placement and university transfer and responding to questions
October	Fall newsletter with admissions time line and focus on faculty members	
December	Spring semester class schedules	
January	Letter with federal financial aid packet	
February	Telephone calls to all prospective students to ask if they have any questions about Cochise College	
March	Spring newsletter with a focus on activities and programs of study	
April	Fall semester class schedules	
June	Fall orientation information for traditional students	Fall orientation information for nontraditional students

to Cochise College or not. Once prospective students become applicants, we send additional information to them.

Making It Work: Final Suggestions

Evaluating an inquiry tracking system is a difficult task, since even the most effective system is at best only a storehouse of data and information. The success of a system depends really upon the way in which information is used. At Cochise Community College we attempt to serve students in a personal way, beginning with their first contact with the college. At the same time, we rely on technology—a computer—and a flexible data base to enable us to provide students with information that meets their needs on a timely basis. As a result of our experience, we offer some admonitions to those planning or revising a prospective student tracking system at community colleges:

- Keep in mind the purpose of the system, and build in data elements that are pertinent to that purpose. An effective tracking system is not a warehouse of everything you can know about a student, nor should it rely on data that students cannot or will not provide.
- Review the system often to ensure that it continues to support office and institutional goals.
- Maintain a free flow of communication among all who work with the system.
- Update the system on a regular basis to keep it current.
- Understand that there will be constant growth and change in the system, and remain flexible.

As colleges face possible enrollment drops during the next few years, it is increasingly important to find ways to attract students. Cochise College has found that a personal touch is appealing. Keeping your admissions office "on track" can be an effective tool for addressing individuals' needs while at the same time managing data effectively.

Reference

Helfgot, S. R. "Opportunities in Diversity." In D. G. Creamer and C. R. Dassance (eds.), *Opportunities for Student Development in Two-Year Colleges.* Columbus, Ohio: National Association of Student Personnel Administrators, 1986.

Alison Rutter Barrett is director of admissions at Cochise College, Douglas, Arizona.

*Few community colleges are sufficiently sophisticated
in collecting, maintaining, and analyzing data for intake
assessment to adequately document basic skills outcomes.*

A Tracking Scheme for Basic Skills Intake Assessment

Richard A. Voorhees, Sharon Hart

It is not surprising that many two-year colleges have found external pressures to assess the basic skills of their incoming students at conflict with their historical admissions policies. To older faculty and staff who have grown up with the community college movement and who have played key roles in actualizing the goal of open access, the thought of posing yet one more hurdle to enrollment for new students is especially burdensome. Campus hesitancy about assessment procedures has been muted by the rising interest of state governing boards and legislatures in measuring institutional effectiveness and students' basic skills functioning. Two-thirds of the fifty states have statewide assessment initiatives on the books, nine states specifically call for basic skills intake assessment, and eight states are examining the issue (Finney and Boyer, 1987). In states where basic skills assessment for community college students is not mandated, the national clarion call soon will be hard to ignore. New intake assessment procedures will need to be developed at the campus level.

Chief among the challenges that community colleges will need to meet within this rapidly changing environment is to trace the effectiveness of their efforts. This chapter provides a brief overview of the construction of a longitudinal tracking system that can be used to address

T. H. Bers (ed.). *Using Student Tracking Systems Effectively.*
New Directions for Community Colleges, no. 66. San Francisco: Jossey-Bass, Summer 1989.

questions of effectiveness. This chapter is not intended to provide guidance to community colleges wishing to document their basic skills outcomes. Although we propose a system that later can serve as a basis for basic skills outcome assessment, the premise of this chapter is that few community colleges are sufficiently sophisticated in collecting, maintaining, and analyzing data for intake assessment to do an adequate job of documenting basic skills outcomes. Careful monitoring and tracking of students participating in basic skills intake assessment must be executed before outcome assessment can be meaningful.

Given the enrollment patterns of typical community college students, the vast majority of whom will not persist to a degree or certificate (see, for example, Walleri, 1981), an institution's opportunity to engage in basic skills outcome studies hinges upon the implementation of a tracking system that is sensitive to the multiplicity of student goals and changing student circumstances. Because of the dynamic nature of clientele served, construction of such a tracking system presents a particular challenge.

One reasonably may argue that there are fewer opportunities to capture the opinions, attitudes, or, indeed, basic skills functioning of students who are in their last term of community college attendance since, unlike baccalaureate-granting institutions, few pass through a predefined exit point. Few would argue that the assessment of completers—that is, those students who got what they came for—is desirable. However, it is beyond the predictive ability of most community colleges to forecast when this point is reached for a given student. How, then, can we distinguish a completer from a student who is likely to just walk away?

The solution to this problem has its roots in the practice of collecting goal-related information from entering students and in establishing mechanisms for updating this information each term. Community college students arrive with goals, articulated or not, that may not match the institution's stated curriculum or mission. In this chapter, we argue that any research conducted in the community college that purports to weigh the effectiveness of student-related programs, especially an evaluation of student outcomes and the effectiveness of an assessment program, will bear a positive relationship to the timeliness with which information about student goals is collected.

Who Should Be Assessed?

One of the first questions a community college must ask is whom do we assess? The logical premise of basic skills intake assessment is to identify those students who are at risk in the curriculum and to place them in classes that match their skill levels. Few among us would consign a particular ethnic group, age group, or sex to assessment testing in lieu of testing all students equally. Although many would argue that part-time or nondegree- (or noncertificate-) seeking students should not be assessed, the pursuit of egalitarianism has resulted in some institutions electing to assess all incoming students. The largest group of institutions in this category is the Los Angeles Community College District, where every entering student is subject to an assessment of his or her basic skills functioning. Some institutions, such as Arapahoe Community College in Colorado, have phased in basic skills intake assessment over a period of years, initially exempting part-time students and those not seeking degrees and certificates, and are now approaching the time when all incoming students will be assessed. Such large-scale cognitive testing programs are costly in both the purchase of testing material and in providing staff resources. However, where legislatures or governing boards have mandated basic skills assessment for all, few alternatives exist.

Where flexibility is possible, the decision of who to assess should reflect the philosophy of the college as it relates to basic skills assessment and should be determined only after careful analyses of historical data. These data, properly assembled and interpreted, can lend credence to the presumption that certain categories of students are more at risk in the curriculum than others and can identify profiles that describe future students who should be assessed. Below, we examine how a longitudinal file can be assembled and discuss how key components of such a file can be used to inform basic skills intake assessment and, later, basic skills outcome assessment.

Construction of an Assessment Data Base

The good news about beginning to do assessment research is that all or almost all of the necessary data have probably already been collected. The bad news is that the data may be scattered throughout the campus. Some data may be on microcomputers, some may be in various files on the mainframe, and much of the data required to build a longitudinal file may be found in file cabinets. It is almost certain that each data source will have a different format or structure. Much effort may be needed to locate and compile available data. At Arapahoe Community College, this process was accomplished in two major steps.

Merging the Data. The first step involved extracting and recoding the data. Student registration files for the fall 1987 term and historical term files for each semester for the past four years were located. A recent software conversion meant that the variables in historical term files shared neither a common format nor coding scheme with the fall 1987 student record file. Further, academic history files for previous terms were also incompatible, necessitating considerable effort to convert and recode both these sets of data files. Because the academic history files included the classes for which students had enrolled and their grades, their accessibility as a freestanding data source was deemed necessary for subsequent analyses of student progress. Results from the college's basic skills assessment were transferred from microcomputer files to the mainframe for merging with the student record files. All data were converted to sequential ASCII files during this step to ensure future transportability among available software packages.

The data for all 6,815 students enrolled for the fall 1987 semester went into a master file for assessment research. Because of its size and disk storage limitations on the mainframe, the resulting master file was stored on tape.

Extracting Longitudinal Files. The second major step involved accessing the master file to extract data to create longitudinal files for tracking purposes. The resulting files contained fewer variables, providing a more convenient means of tracking a defined student cohort. Variables included in the longitudinal files are found in Table 1 and are categorized as either fixed or variable elements. Fixed elements are collected, usually once, from student registration records and contain information that is not expected to change during the course of a student's enrollment. Variable elements are term-specific and contain information that can change from term to term.

Dynamics of File Building

The longitudinal model presented in Table 1 is initiated in a given term and either is assembled during future terms or is assembled from available data collected in previous terms, in a process similar to that described above. Although the former method provides a basis for comparing retention and class completion rates to inform student selection criteria for basic skills assessment, it suffers from the fact that scores on basic skills measures are likely to be missing because of the short history of campuswide assessment. Similarly, not all institutions collect the breadth of information suggested here, and this information may be impossible to obtain for past terms. Of course, moving the data collection forward in time eliminates this problem. In either case, however, the college may need to collect special indicator variables: handicapped status, learning disability status, work status, economic disability status, and student goal status, which may depart significantly from current data collection procedures.

A central feature of the longitudinal model is its dependence on student goal information that is collected each term and is treated, along with work status and economic disability status, as a variable element. Variable elements reflect the diversity of student intentions upon entry and necessitate updating the file each term. Foreknowledge of student

Table 1. A Longitudinal Tracking File for Community College Basic Skills Intake Assessment (Proposed Model)

Data Element	Position	Length	Type
Fixed Elements			
Social Security number	1–9	9	N
Birthdate [mmddyy]	10–16	6	N
Sex	17	1	AN
Race/ethnicity	18	1	AN
Previous education	19–20	2	N
Handicapped flag	21	1	AN
Learning disability flag	22	1	AN
Reading score	23–24	2	N
Mathematics score	25–26	2	N
English usage score	27–28	2	N

Variable Elements	*Term 1*	*Term 2*	*Term 3* ...	*Term 8*
Hours attempted	29–30	39–40	49–50	99–100
Hours completed	31–32	41–42	51–52	101–102
Cumulative GPA	33–34	43–44	53–54	103–104
Student goal	35	45	55	105
Work status [ft, pt, none]	36	46	56	106
Economic disability flag	37	47	57	107
Goal attained flag	38	48	58	108

goals, in particular, allows the college to state with confidence whether a given student has attained his or her goal in a given term and provides the opportunity to articulate institutional outcomes from a student perspective.

Establishing Cohorts. Initially, institutions may wish to include all new students who have taken basic skills tests within one large file. After their first term, students can be assigned to cohorts based on their academic history. The number of cohorts a community college elects to track probably should not exceed ten and should be established based on distinct behavioral patterns that separate cohort membership (Ewell, 1987). These behavioral patterns can include persistence and credit-hour completion rates. Completion of prescribed basic skills classes may also be a useful cross-cutting variable.

Advantages. The chief advantage of creating longitudinal data files is that they may represent the only opportunity that institutions have to track student performance. Transactional software packages found on most mainframe computers store and maintain student data so that academic history files are continually updated. New information is written over old values for grade point average, hours attempted, and hours completed each term. Consequently, it may not be possible to track a given student's academic progress across more than one term.

Disadvantages. Longitudinal files pose two distinct problems. First, term files contain information that cannot be updated after it is captured. At most institutions, data are usually captured on the institution's census date for reporting purposes. Significant changes may occur in student intentions, economic status, and work status between the census date and the end of a term. These changes may be unknown and can affect subsequent analysis. Second, term files are difficult to link together without special expertise. SPSS-X and SAS are powerful software packages and can accomplish multiple mergers of term files, but they require knowledge of computer operating systems and data file procedures that call for relative user sophistication.

In the model proposed in Table 1, the reader will note that certain data from academic history files—that is, course enrollment, grades in courses, and student major information—are not present. Their absence in Table 1 reflects a desire to limit the longitudinal file to manageable proportions. These data elements can be retrieved from the freestanding academic history files, however, should more finite analysis of course completion rates, changes in majors, or progress in described portions of the curriculum become necessary or desirable.

Maintaining Files. Maintenance of the longitudinal file in subsequent terms is accomplished by adding new information to the end of each record. The model suggested here covers an eight-term span, although institutional experience may dictate that the length of time for which a longitudinal model is developed be shorter or longer. Ewell (1987) suggests that a reasonable rule of thumb is that point in which 90 percent of the cohort has either graduated or has not enrolled for a specified period of time. Institutions will have to determine whether to include their summer sessions within the time period covered by the model.

The college's computer center will find that updating the longitudinal file twice a term (once at the institution's census date to collect current information on work status, economic disability, and student goal status, and again at the end of the term to collect hours completed and GPA) to be a relatively simple process once the file has been created. Data for students who are not present during a subsequent term will be blank in the corresponding columns, a condition that SPSS-X can incorporate within user analyses.

Range of Analysis

Particularly important in the analysis of the effectiveness of basic skills intake assessment are retention studies and academic performance profiles. That is, can it be demonstrated that certain cohorts of students who have been placed in classes based on basic skills assessment persist better, have lower withdrawal rates in certain classes, or earn significantly higher grades than other students?

Retention data, by themselves, probably do little to illuminate the potential effectiveness of intake assessment. In tandem with individual grade point average data, however, a somewhat clearer picture begins to emerge. Grade point average data and credit-hour completion rates can be used to identify the point where students are experiencing difficulty and can trigger an analysis of course enrollment, subsequent grades, and other information linked to the longitudinal file through the academic history file. Caution must be used in these analyses to factor for grade inflation and withdrawal for other than academic reasons. For community colleges, the term *withdrawal* has never enjoyed an unambiguous definition. Moreover, where the disproportionate majority of grades awarded by an institution are in the *A* or *B* range, or records are not maintained for the reasons students report for withdrawal from class or college, the validity of research findings merit careful examination. A fair method for discriminating among students who are truly at risk would incorporate a complete picture of academic data coupled with those background variables that are thought to affect success.

Summary

Obviously, the amount of information contained in the longitudinal file proposed in this chapter can inform more than assessment research and easily can extend to other research projects including retention analyses, withdrawal studies, course enrollment patterns, and grading studies. Each of these research projects might fit well under the rubric of assessment, but they also represent long-standing questions that were difficult to address for many colleges without the immediate availability of these data.

Recent national interest in institutional effectiveness means that the participation by community colleges that heretofore have not been involved in basic skills assessment is probably inevitable. The way in which colleges choose to collect, analyze, and report basic skills data also is likely to be an area of increased attention. In Texas, for example, a consortium of community colleges recently has begun to develop a common tracking system in conjunction with the National Center for Higher Education Management Systems (Ewell, Parker, and Jones, 1988). This system, known as the Longitudinal Student Tracking and Reporting (LONESTAR) system, is described in Chapter Nine of this volume.

It is probable that other states will look toward construction of longitudinal tracking systems to measure community college effectiveness, in general, and basic skills effectiveness, in particular. This may be an encouraging development as governing boards, legislators, and other decision makers move away from one-shot analyses of program effectiveness and seek new ways to address the unique needs and characteristics of community college students.

References

Ewell, P. T. "Principles of Longitudinal Enrollment Analysis: Conducting Retention and Student Flow Studies." In J. A. Muffo and G. W. McLaughlin (eds.), *A Primer on Institutional Research.* Tallahassee, Fla.: Association for Institutional Research, 1987.

Ewell, P. T., Parker, R., and Jones, D. P. *Establishing a Longitudinal Student Tracking System: An Implementation Handbook.* Boulder, Colo.: National Center for Higher Education Management Systems, 1988.

Finney, J. E., and Boyer, C. M. *Individual State Profiles. Assessment and Outcomes Measurement: A View from the States.* Denver, Colo.: Education Commission of the States, 1987.

Walleri, R. D. *Student Retention and Attrition in the Community College: A Review and Research Design.* Gresham, Ore.: Mount Hood Community Colleges, 1981. 37 pp. (ED 210 064)

Richard A. Voorhees is dean of student affairs at Black Hills State College, Spearfish, South Dakota.

Sharon Hart is director of planning and research at Arapahoe Community College, Littleton, Colorado.

Collaboration between the data processing center and the developmental studies program at one community college resulted in efficient monitoring of the progress of underprepared students.

Computerized Tracking System for Underprepared Students

Pat Smittle, Michael R. LaVallee, Jr., William E. Carman

As open-door institutions, community colleges enroll many students whose academic skills are insufficient to enable them to successfully complete college credit classes. The assessment of basic skills, placement of students into courses, and subsequent tracking of their progress vary from college to college, and state to state. This chapter will describe a computer tracking system for underprepared students at one community college. Located in a state that has placed increasing emphasis on requiring students to remediate basic skills deficiencies before proceeding with college-level work, Santa Fe Community College (SFCC) has revised its tracking system several times to meet growing internal needs for accurate and timely data and in response to state mandates.

An Overview of Santa Fe Community College

Established by the Florida state legislature in 1965 as a comprehensive community college with an open-door policy, Santa Fe Community Col-

T. H. Bers (ed.). *Using Student Tracking Systems Effectively.*
New Directions for Community Colleges, no. 66. San Francisco: Jossey-Bass, Summer 1989.

lege is located in a predominantly rural area of north central Florida with a population of about 206,500. The college operates two sites: its main campus on a 125-acre tract of land in northwest Gainesville and an instructional center in the town of Starke, approximately thirty miles northeast of Gainesville. A new instructional center located in an area shopping mall began operation in the winter of 1988. Santa Fe Community College is one of the primary feeder colleges to the University of Florida, which is located in Gainesville.

In the fall of 1987 a record 9,210 students were enrolled in college credit courses, with another 5,000 students enrolled in community education programs. The majority of students are enrolled in the associate of arts transfer curriculum, although the college also offers vocational-technical courses that lead to degrees or certificates, and community education courses for lifelong learning.

Santa Fe Community College's mission, as stated in the college's 1987 catalogue, is "to offer its students the opportunity to develop their intellectual capacities, occupational aptitudes, and avocational interests while contributing to the student's personal growth and to contemporary society's need for informed, concerned, and responsive citizens" (p. 10).

Underprepared Students at SFCC

Early Attempts at Assessment, Placement, and Tracking. Since its inception, Santa Fe Community College has firmly held to the commitment to equal access and opportunity for all persons. Consequently, the college has underwritten major efforts aimed at maximizing students' chances to fulfill their goals. These efforts are most clearly demonstrated in the area of underprepared students, estimated to comprise at least 50 percent of the entering freshmen.

During the college's early years of operation, the skills of entering students were not assessed, and all students enrolled directly in college-level courses. Underprepared students were encouraged to seek assistance in a lab setting after their instructors recognized skill deficiencies that would hamper college-level work. Since this system relied totally on the students' initiative to seek the recommended academic support, it was woefully inadequate because few of those students who needed help would follow through with the teacher recommendation and there was no system for follow-up. Ultimately, however, the need for more formal mechanisms for identifying underprepared students and providing them with needed assistance became apparent to college personnel. Various assessment and teaching models were designed, tested, and modified within the developmental studies area.

Mandatory Assessment and Placement. In 1981 the college adopted a required assessment and placement policy, and the need for additional support for underprepared students became even greater. The developmental studies program recognized that the new policy meant greater accountability for student performance and began to develop a computerized tracking system. Thus began a six-year collaboration between the college's data processing center, which operates and maintains the institution's mainframe computer, and the developmental studies program.

The goals of the initial version of the computerized tracking system were efficient monitoring of the progress of underprepared students and accurate statistical information. For the developmental studies administration, the tracking system monitored students' progress during their tenure in developmental courses and supplied statistics to generate required reports that focused on numbers of students enrolled and passing rates of students in all developmental studies courses. Academic advisers were able to use the assessment information to direct students into the appropriate courses at the beginning of their college careers. Unfortunately, the design contained a weakness that allowed students with low assessment test scores or students who had failed developmental courses to register for college-level courses before demonstrating competency in the deficient basic skills area.

The need for an enforcement tool within the computerized tracking system became clear. Many possibilities were considered, including integrating the tracking system program with the registration program, which would give the computer the capability of locking students out of the usual registration process until they had fulfilled their basic skills requirements. Because of the concern that integration would create unmanageable registration problems, it was not considered to be a viable option at that time. The manual checking of student records, a system already in place, was continued. As an enforcement tool, it was a slow, inefficient method of administering the institution's policy.

Enter . . . the State. In 1985 the Florida legislature and State Board of Education set statewide standards in the basic skills areas. Rule 6A-10.315: College Preparatory Testing, Placement, and Instruction states, in part: "First-time-in-college applicants for admission to community colleges and universities who intend to enter degree programs shall be tested prior to the completion of registration, using one (1) or more tests listed herein, and, effective the 1985 fall term, shall enroll in college preparatory communication and computation instruction if the test scores are below those listed herein" (*Florida Administrative Code Annotated,* 1986, p. 441).

Other sections of the State Board of Education rule name the acceptable assessment tests, set definitive competency scores in the basic skills areas, define the competency parameters, and establish the maximum number of terms allowed for a student to successfully complete the college preparatory instruction.

The state mandate served as a catalyst that prompted Santa Fe Community College to revise both its developmental studies program and its tracking of underprepared students. The developmental studies program was renamed the college prep program and was expanded to include elements of student orientation, academic advisement, basic skills remediation, and career counseling. A simple premise was adopted by the college prep program as its most important guideline: awareness is the first step toward remediation. A college prep advisement team consisting of a full-time professional specialist and two part-time employees provides continuity between the varied elements of the program and assures compliance with the state mandate. The college prep staff now includes an administrator, ten full-time faculty members, three full-time professional specialists, and five full-time career service employees as well as several part-time faculty members and aides.

What does the state mandate mean to underprepared students? It means that prior to their initial registration they must take an assessment test, and if test scores indicate basic skills deficiencies in reading, writing, mathematics, or a combination of the three, the students must meet with a member of the college prep advisement team. The relationship between test scores and the college prep program is explained and the students are assisted in registering properly for the first semester of study. Registration in courses designed to correct basic skills deficiencies is required, although students may concurrently register for college-level courses that are not within the discipline of the basic skills deficiency.

Early in the first semester, a member of the college prep advisement team visits all college prep classes to reinforce information that was presented at students' initial meetings. Subsequently students, with the help of a member of the college prep advisement team, plan their next semester of work. During these individual meetings, academic requirements for various careers are discussed, and after minimal counseling, students may be referred to other areas of the college for specialized counseling and program planning. This process of academic advisement, registration, and monitoring is continued until students have met all basic skills requirements. Keeping track of students as they move through the institution and complete basic skills requirements is a key element of the revised student tracking system.

Computerized Student Tracking System, Revised

The 1985 state mandate for assessment, placement, and remediation, and the college's expanded program for providing this academic assistance to students, were supported by a demand for greater accountability. The parameters of the existing tracking system had to be redefined, and its method of implementation revised. A revised and expanded tracking system was needed that would be able to handle the registration process for underprepared students and to monitor their progress from initial registration to graduation. The earlier proposal to integrate the tracking system program and the registration program was reexamined and adopted. This revision was carefully designed and placed into operation so the interaction of the programs would not increase the usual student frustration during the rush of registration.

Two major improvements were made to the tracking system: the early identification of underprepared students who had failed developmental courses and the monitoring of developmental students after they had completed the college prep program and had progressed to key college-level courses. The former brought to the college prep advisement team the ability to intervene at early stages of students' educational programs. The latter supplied the facts and figures needed to generate required State Board of Education reports that addressed the effectiveness of the legislative mandate.

Most Essential Element. The most essential element of the computerized tracking system is its capability to ensure that students register in accordance with the requirements of the state legislature. To attain this, the data processing center capitalized on the computer's ability to generate flags that then force the computer to make "logical" decisions.

For example, a student's assessment score indicates a basic skills deficiency in mathematics. When his assessment score is entered into the computer, a flag (in this example the flag would be the letter M) is automatically placed into his record by the computer. Should an attempt be made to register this student in a college-level mathematics course, the computer would recognize the M flag and lock the student out until the required developmental course is entered into the computer. When lockout occurs, the computer's terminal screen displays a message informing the student that he is required to meet with a member of the college prep advisement team before his registration can be continued. At the meeting, the cycle of academic advisement, registration, and monitoring, which the college prep advisement team conducts, is begun. This process guarantees registration in the required developmental course while allowing concurrent registration in college-level work in areas that are not affected by the skill deficiency. Each skill area has a unique letter flag: W for writing, R for reading, and M for mathematics. Other letter flags, such as X and P, are used to monitor the progress of students.

The inherent benefit of using flags to track students is that they facilitate early intervention by the college prep advisement team. In its mandate, the state legislature decreed that a student was to be permitted a maximum of three terms in each basic skills area to remediate basic skills deficiencies. In light of the three-term limitation, early intervention becomes essential. Students who are experiencing minimal success in their remedial work can be provided with timely, individualized counseling during which they may reexamine their priorities or explore other paths for success before the college's open door must be closed.

Contents

Mainframe computers operated by integrated programs, such as the computerized tracking system program, can manipulate and combine elements from existing data bases, thus effectively eliminating the time-consuming chore of double and triple data entry. In its present form, not only does the computerized tracking system extract the needed information from computerized student records that were created during the application and assessment processes, but required additions, deletions, and modifications to the student records are done by the computer as the student progresses through the program. For example, the registration flag is automatically removed when a passing grade is entered on the student record.

The contents of the system—students' names and Social Security numbers, first term of enrollment, assessment scores, deficient skills area flags, and enrollment history, to name a few elements—provide simple, quantitative data for program evaluation. These data can be accessed from on-line terminals or computer printouts.

The raw quantitative data that serve as the basis for the computer tracking system are available via terminals to all college personnel that have access to student records. The computer tracking system printouts are made available to the chairman of the developmental studies program after she and the computer systems analyst engage in careful deliberation regarding the specific needs and purposes for the report.

Value of Tracking System: Beyond Expectations

When the computerized tracking system at Santa Fe Community College was conceived, its primary functions were to monitor the progress of underprepared students and to supply pertinent data for accountability reports. But during its six-year existence, as it efficiently performed the two primary functions, its sphere of value as a college prep program management tool unexpectedly expanded into the areas of academic advisement and registration, accurate student placement, and program evaluation.

Assessment scores, registration flags, courses attempted, and course grades from the tracking system provide the college prep team with current data to use in advising and registering students who are enrolled in the program. On-line terminals are located in the developmental studies offices for advisement and limited registration purposes. The same capabilities for the college prep advisement team are made available in the registration area during regularly scheduled college registration periods.

At Santa Fe Community College, formative evaluation of the college prep program is an ongoing activity, and elements of the tracking system supply the data that address the evaluation criteria. For example, the tracking system provides the following:

- Number of students registered in college prep courses
- Performance of students in college prep courses
- Number of former college prep students registered in required college-level courses in mathematics, English, and humanities
- Performance of former college prep students in key college-level courses
- Graduation dates of former college prep students.

Evaluations are routinely conducted at the end of each semester, and they often serve as the impetus for curriculum revisions, grading policy changes, and updating of the institutional model to facilitate program improvements. Recently this was reflected in the upgrading of the developmental studies writing curriculum after the tracking system report revealed that most students who had earned a grade lower than B did not succeed in the following English course.

Final Observations

Valuable college resources were expended to develop the sophisticated computerized tracking system that the college prep program presently uses. Is such an effort justified? Since the computerized tracking system is presently providing the college prep program with accurate information that enables it to move steadily toward its goal of enhancing the postsecondary educational success of underprepared students, the answer is yes. Can the system be improved? Of course it can. It is a system that was molded and shaped by administrators and support personnel to fill their needs for information, and improvements can always be made.

Finally, Santa Fe Community College's heavy reliance on the speed and efficiency of the computer should not be misinterpreted. The college has not removed the human factor from student contact, nor will it ever.

References

Florida Administrative Code Annotated. Vol. 3. Sect. 6A-10.3015. Norcross, Ga.: Harrison, 1986, p. 441.

Pat Smittle is chairman of learning labs and developmental studies at Santa Fe Community College, Gainesville, Florida.

Michael R. LaVallee, Jr., is the computer lab manager in the learning lab developmental studies program at Santa Fe Community College.

William E. Carman is a senior computer systems analyst in the data processing center at Santa Fe Community College.

An effective tracking and monitoring system must have the potential to facilitate students' effectiveness and efficient participation in their education from enrollment to graduation.

Tracking and Monitoring Students in Special Groups

Melvin L. Gay, Costas S. Boukouvalas

This chapter discusses a tracking and monitoring approach for special students as it is presently implemented at Central Piedmont Community College. The system was developed as a response to the college's open-door policy and its desire to serve the underserved populations.

Central Piedmont Community College is a student-oriented, urban institution known for its continuing innovation and quality of instruction. In 1985 it was named in the top five in teaching excellence among the nation's 1,200 community colleges. The college "is committed to the concept that, given enough time, most students can accomplish any learning task" (*Central Piedmont Community College Catalogue*, 1986–88, p. 49). Consequently, the institution provides ample opportunities for students to learn at varying rates, a nonpunitive grading system, and individualized control of the rates of learning.

Through the nonpunitive grading system students may receive an *A*, *B*, or *C*, based on the completed course objectives. When the minimum objectives are not met, some students may receive an *IM* (incomplete make-up). This will allow them to complete the predetermined objectives. An *IR* (incomplete repeat) is given to students who have not made any considerable progress, allowing them to reenroll.

The individualized control of the rates of learning allows students to

T. H. Bers (ed.). *Using Student Tracking Systems Effectively.*
New Directions for Community Colleges, no. 66. San Francisco: Jossey-Bass, Summer 1989.

48

work on different course units and at different degrees of effort. One student may work on unit five, while another is on unit ten, and they each may spend as many hours as they need. Through this approach the motivated and better prepared student may move on and complete the course, while the underprepared student may require more time and additional assistance.

Since 1971 the college has provided a comprehensive support services program to the hearing, visually, and physically impaired, the learning disabled, substance abusers, high school dropouts, single parents, and students with limited English-speaking abilities. These are the groups that we consider to be special populations. They are high-risk students and they lack preparation, college and social skills, motivation, and persistence. The tracking and monitoring system discussed in this chapter is directed to these groups.

The department of student support services is staffed by three counselors, two program coordinators, a senior interpreter, a tutorial services coordinator, seven full-time interpreters, and a number of part-time interpreters, tutors, notetakers, and readers. Each employee is assigned to serve students from one of the special groups or disabilities and to work in cooperation with other personnel when they deal with multihandicapped students.

Figure 1. Organization Chart for Department of Student Support Services, Central Piedmont Community College, Charlotte, North Carolina

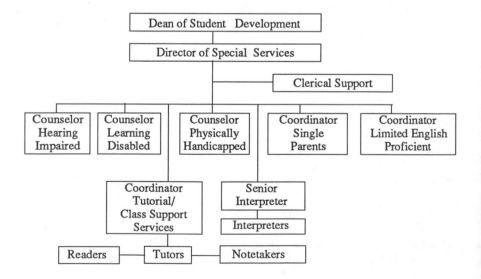

The department serves an average of 35 hearing impaired, 85 learning disabled, 130 physically handicapped, 150 low-income (neediest) single parents, and 250 limited English proficient students.

Frequently, student support services such as orientation, advising, counseling, peer tutoring, and tracking are evaluated based on their "relation to institutional holding power" (Creamer, 1980, p. 11). An effective student tracking and monitoring system must possess the potential for "holding power," which is defined in this chapter as the ability of the system to facilitate students' effective and efficient participation in their education from enrollment to graduation. Effectiveness refers to proper course and curriculum placement, and to meaningful participation in college life. Efficiency refers to the time or duration required for students to complete their studies.

Central Piedmont Community College, as many other open-door institutions, abides by the principle that having the opportunity and the proper support, students can accomplish any learning task. The open-door colleges provide an opportunity for the underprepared, the academically limited, and the culturally deprived to pursue postsecondary education. However, they frequently encounter a "revolving door."

Underprepared students continue to fail, and we erroneously lead them to believe that they did not fail but they did not have sufficient time to complete their work. Eventually, as their persistence weakens, they become dropout statistics. Therefore, a comprehensive student tracking and monitoring system must provide continuous support and follow-up from enrollment to graduation. It must prevent the high dropout rate that is typical of these special groups.

Most of the special populations at Central Piedmont Community College are served by the support services department, which is designed to provide for the students' educational effectiveness and efficiency. The student tracking and monitoring system discussed in this chapter is the vehicle through which this is realized.

Role of the Computer

Our educational system is known for its fascination with technology. Educators welcomed simple teaching machines of the past as well as sophisticated computers of our time with excitement and fear. Excitement was prompted because we believed we found an answer to ineffectiveness in teaching, and fear was the result of the concern that teachers might be replaced by equipment. Today we are no longer afraid of the computer, but we believe that it can do everything with little effort on our part.

We read that "a Computerized Academic Monitoring System was especially designed and implemented to increase the retention and graduation rates . . . of students" (Goodrich, 1980–81, p. 87). Elsewhere, we read of a "new computer model that tracks all the changes . . . made by students and tabulates the data . . . to facilitate analysis" (Simpson, 1987, p. 323).

These and numerous other discussions do not tell us what happens to the student. Many computer tracking and monitoring systems are "designed to do nothing more than tabulate and format the major changes made by a student" (Simpson, 1987, p. 325) and to provide information for the benefit not of the student but the institution.

The computerized student tracking system stores static information obtained at different stages, which only communicates what has happened. A truly dynamic tracking and monitoring system must provide information on how students are doing now and how we can change the behavior of students to promote the successful completion of their goals.

It is only human involvement that can provide us with vital information on student attendance, class involvement, and student academic problems. It is only human involvement that can immediately utilize this information to change the behavior of students and the outcome. The human involvement of a counselor is necessary to keep in constant contact with the students and their teachers.

Institutional Commitment

Central Piedmont Community College maintains a sophisticated computer support system. The computer is used for telephone and on-line registration and will restrict the student from entering into a course without the necessary prerequisites or appropriate scores on placement tests. It maintains class rosters, student schedules, grades, credits, and other important data needed for day-to-day institutional operations.

The present tracking and monitoring system was developed over a period of years as a response to a number of factors that were encountered in the college's efforts to serve the special groups listed previously. The first factor was the college's commitment and basic operational philosophy to serve all segments of the population in its service area, including students with special needs.

The second major factor began to be influential in 1971, when the college introduced a comprehensive program to meet the educational needs of the disabled. This commitment was made six years before Section 504 of the Vocational Rehabilitation Act became law. During the first years of this program, the instructional staff were ambivalent, pleased that the college had made this commitment but concerned about their lack of experience and knowledge in serving the disabled.

The third and only external factor was the demand by sponsoring agencies, such as the North Carolina Division of Vocational Rehabilitation, the North Carolina Services for the Blind, and others, to see that their clients receive services. Clients were required to complete their studies in the period stipulated in the college catalogue. Only two quarters were allowed for the completion of any remedial work, forcing the college to be effective and efficient in its services to these special groups.

The combination of these three factors motivated the development and implementation of the present tracking and monitoring system, whose components are briefly described here.

Preenrollment College Visits. The college recognizes that each college, like each student, has a unique personality. Research indicates that student-institution "fit" is an important factor in student success (Moos, 1979). Therefore, the support services department encourages students, especially those from outside the immediate area, to visit the college. During the visit they are able to tour the campus facilities, meet with their counselor and other students, and receive an orientation to the available support services. At this time the counselor will open folders for the students.

Assessment. During assessment our goal is to get to know the students by gathering a variety of data about their psychological, social, and academic skills, as well as to identify concerns they may express verbally or those that can be intuited by counselors and others. Among the concerns of special populations are the availability of such communication aids as sign language, large-print books, and braille documents; ease of access to mobility around the campus; extent of family support; child care; and transportation needs. The data gathered from the assessment are entered into the students' files and the counselor begins to identify and locate the needed resources.

Orientation. New students attend a day-long orientation designed to allow the students to make any last minute arrangement with housing and registration and to meet other students.

Academic Placement. The student's readiness, the instructor's attitude, and the ability of the institution to provide sufficient academic support are key factors affecting proper placement in courses. In addition, the counselor must take into account the information obtained from the assessment and the results of any placement tests that the student has completed.

Instructor Contacts. The staff of the support services department see themselves as partners with the student and the instructor in the learning process. Further, it is believed that the instructor must know as much as possible about the student. Therefore, with the student's prior approval, a letter is forwarded to each instructor giving the student's disability or learning problem, the student's most effective learning style, and recommended instructional approaches. With this memo counselors are introduced to instructors and make themselves available to help when needed.

Informal Contact. The support services staff are encouraged to maintain continuous contact with the instructional staff. Such contacts may be held in the hallways, in the instructors' offices, during coffee breaks, and in other settings. Counselors may ask for permission to make classroom and lab visits to identify possible negative reinforcers, which Darkenwald and Gavin (1987) argue are among the most potent predictors of dropping out.

End-of-Quarter Assessment and Registration. At the end of each quarter the student and counselor meet to discuss the student's performance and to select courses for the following quarter. At this meeting they assess the support services available during the previous quarter, and they determine what services will be required in the next one. If the student had difficulties, plans are made on how to avoid similar situations the following quarter.

Placement. The last component of this system is placement. The support services staff who are directly involved consider placement (college and work) as the culmination of their efforts and the students' ultimate goal. Placement for this system starts on the first day of enrollment. Students are taught to understand the relationship between class attendance and proper work habits, the importance of social skills, and the need for development of independent skills.

Tracking and monitoring of students continues with the student's initial employment or college placement. The student's counselor may conduct visits on the employment site to communicate with employers and with the student's new counselor after transfer. The counselors are interested in finding out to what extent the student was properly prepared for work and/or college, and how the findings can be incorporated into the available services.

System Characteristics

The success of the system for tracking and monitoring special population students at Central Piedmont Community College is due in large part to general and direct involvement by student services staff, instructors, and the students themselves, and to clarity in communications.

Involvement. Involvement here is defined as the amount of time and energy students, support staff, and instructional staff devote to their relationships as they relate to the learning process. The monitoring system allows students to play an active role in their learning.

Clarity of Communication. Students at risk do not have tolerance for ambiguity. They expect very clear communication of responsibilities and expectations. Students from these special groups who perceive the environment to be confused, uncertain, and unpredictable may choose the quickest way out, which is total withdrawal from college. In addition, changes must be handled carefully. We have found that students must receive sufficient time and opportunity before a change is implemented.

Comprehensive Records. The counselors maintain a number of records to allow them to track and monitor the progress of students. The counselors have a folder for each student in their office where a complete record is kept. Use of these records is restricted to the counselors and their clerical support because the records may contain confidential information. In addition to the student's individual folder, the counselors maintain an index card that contains the student's address, class schedule, teachers' names, vocational rehabilitation counselor, child-care center, and so on. Finally, the counselors have quick access to the mainframe computer through a terminal located in their office area.

Evaluation. Although we do not have clear quantitative data resulting from research with experimental and control groups, we have other factors that indicate the success of the system. Some of these factors are as follows:

1. Retention and completion among disabled students have doubled within the last five years.

2. Course completions among all special populations have risen to 70 percent.

3. Teachers' requests for in-class and out-of-class assistance have doubled.

4. Response time to teacher requests for assistance has changed from days to hours.

5. Performance of students who transfer to four-year institutions is equal to, or in some cases better than, those who enrolled as freshmen.

6. Retention of single parents has increased from 21 percent to approximately 73 percent.

7. Class attendance among all special groups has remained between 80 and 85 percent.

8. Degree of satisfaction among students and staff is very high. Comments by students such as "People are so involved with you," "I was totally elated with my experience there," "Everybody was there to help you," and an instructor's statement that "I called about a blind student and within an hour I had four people from your department in my office" are clear indicators of the success and potential of this tracking and monitoring system.

Summary

This discussion was based on the assumption that open-door institutions admit students from special populations who may be unprepared academically and socially to engage in college studies and who require nurturing "until they are ready to hold their own" (Vas, 1987, p. 29). To provide nurturing there must be a well-developed system of support services, extensive involvement by students and staff, and clarity in commu-

54

nications at every level. Therefore, continuous human involvement is an important factor for the success of both the high-risk student and the tracking and monitoring system.

References

Central Piedmont Community College Catalogue. Springfield, Ill.: Phillips Brothers, 1986-88, p. 49.

Creamer, D. G. "Educational Advising for Student Retention: An Institutional Perspective." *Community College Review,* 1980, 7 (4), 11–16.

Darkenwald, G. G., and Gavin, W. J. "Dropout as a Function of Discrepancies Between Expectations and Actual Experiences of the Classroom Social Environment." *Adult Education Quarterly,* 1987, 37 (3), 152–163.

Goodrich, A. "Computerized Academic Monitoring System: A Support System for Improving Minority Student Persistence in Select Problem Courses." *Journal of Educational Technology Systems,* 1980-81, 9 (2), 87–93.

Moos, R. H. *Evaluating Educational Environments: Procedures, Measures, Findings, and Policy Implications.* San Francisco: Jossey-Bass, 1979.

Simpson, W. A. "Tracking Students Through Majors: Methodology and Applications." *Journal of Higher Education,* 1987, 58 (3), 323–343.

Vas, K. "Building Retention Systems for Talented Minority Students Attending White Universities." *Negro Educational Review,* 1987, 38 (1), 23–29.

Melvin L. Gay is dean for student development at Central Piedmont Community College in Charlotte, North Carolina.

Costas S. Boukouvalas is presently the director of special services at Central Piedmont Community College, Charlotte, North Carolina.

This chapter examines the efforts of Oakton College to track and communicate with students in academic difficulty.

Tracking Students in Community Colleges: The Unreported Challenges

Trudy H. Bers, Alan M. Rubin

The need to track students in community colleges is now widely accepted among college administrators, faculty and boards, and state education officials. The benefits of tracking are many, including but not limited to obtaining information about students' academic progress and achievements, classifying and sending targeted communications to students who exhibit certain characteristics or behaviors, identifying programs or courses in which retention and completion are either problematic or well above expectations, and making direct contacts with students to offer academic as well as other types of assistance.

The logistics of tracking and communicating with community college students are not nearly as simple as outlining the benefits of doing so. In this chapter we examine the efforts of Oakton College to track and communicate with students at those times when they experience academic difficulty and are placed on one of four academic sanctions.

We will present only a simple description of the systems—computer and human—we use and concentrate instead on the actual obstacles we have encountered. Because our student body differs little from the population of students at numerous community colleges throughout the

T. H. Bers (ed.). *Using Student Tracking Systems Effectively.*
New Directions for Community Colleges, no. 66. San Francisco: Jossey-Bass, Summer 1989.

nation, we are confident that the problems we encounter are replicated in many other places.

In describing the obstacles we have faced in tracking and working with students in academic difficulty, we include several brief case studies of students whose academic record, on the surface and as interpreted by the computer program, indicated they were in academic difficulty. In working with these students on a personal basis, however, it was apparent that in some instances a student was not by any definition in academic difficulty. Rather, there were exigencies that interfered with the student following the college's normative calendar for academic progress. The case studies illustrate the inherent problems in applying computer logic to interpreting the meaning of human behavior.

The College: Academic Standards and Tracking

Oakton College is located in the northern suburbs of Chicago and serves a population of some 435,000. The college enrolls 9,100 students (4,200 FTE) in credit courses and approximately another 13,000 per semester in noncredit classes. Founded in 1970, the college was committed to a philosophy of student development that supported a nonpunitive grading system; voluntary assessment testing and course placements; an open door for as long as a student wished to attend, regardless of performance or progress; and a supportive environment in which the student was able to choose courses and curricula according to interest, with little regard to academic abilities to succeed in those courses or curricula.

Academic Standards. In the early 1980s the college's philosophy shifted, and faculty and staff began to be much more directive in their dealings with students. Still committed to helping students make choices, the college began to see that in order to help students succeed, the institution needed to test and place students in basic skill areas commensurate with the students' abilities, to identify and intervene with students who encountered academic failure, and to become more rigorous in articulating and adhering to high academic standards.

A specific manifestation of the revised philosophy was implemented in 1984, when the college adopted its Standards of Academic Progress (SOAP) system. Similar to the system at Miami–Dade, SOAP identifies students who fail to earn a 2.0 (*C*) average or who fail to successfully complete (earn credit in) more than half their courses in a term. The latter criterion is known as the half-course rule. As part of the SOAP system, an *F* grade was instituted.

Multiple semesters of performance below SOAP levels result in a student being placed on warning, then probation, then suspension, and finally, being dismissed. The system applies to all students who have attempted at least twelve credits, regardless of the student's age, academic intent, full- or part-time status, or prior academic history. A complex series of computer programs and computer-generated letters supports the SOAP system.

The SOAP policy stipulates a period during which a student can withdraw from a course without that course being included in SOAP calculations. When a student simply stops attending a class prior to midterm but does not formally withdraw, the faculty member assigns an *N*. The *N* is included in determining the percent of courses completed but does not count in grade point average calculations. Both students and faculty have experienced confusion in understanding the role of the *N* in calculating academic status.

Tracking. Taken together, the practices associated with the college's changing philosophy regarding academic standards prompted an extensive set of efforts to track and communicate with students. However, the notion of a specific system for tracking at Oakton is probably misleading. We have a number of modes of tracking students, some of which rely primarily on in-house student records, some of which depend on information provided from outside agencies (for example, senior institutions), and some of which focus on alumni surveys that are affected by the usual research questions related to response rates, anonymity of responses, vagaries of students' memories, and so on.

In this chapter we draw upon our experience in attempting to track and communicate with students in academic difficulty, although many of the lessons we have learned and issues with which we are struggling are pertinent to more comprehensive tracking and communication processes as well.

Students: Tracking the Elusive "Model"

As we began to discuss, plan, and implement our new academic standards and tracking initiatives, we hypothesized a number of "model" student types: (1) traditional students, whether full- or part-time, who enrolled in contiguous semesters and whose academic achievements consistently put them above the SOAP minimum levels; (2) students who failed to meet academic standards in contiguous terms and who proceeded in linear fashion through warning, probation, suspension, and dismissal; and (3) students whose academic records were more erratic—who met minimum standards in some terms and failed to do so in others. These classifications enabled us to target and sharpen the computer programs we wrote, policies and practices we developed, and letters we sent.

Also shaping our work were a number of implicit assumptions that we began to examine only after some of the difficulties of implementation became severe. These included the following:

- Students adhere to the college calendar; they register, withdraw, and make up incompletes by published deadlines.

- Students read and understand policies about academic standards, and certainly they read their mail carefully and follow directions when the content pertains to their own academic standing.
- If we mail communications to students' addresses, the letters will reach them.
- Certain words, such as *register*, have only one meaning, and that meaning is clear to everyone.
- Faculty understand the use of the *N* indicator and the requirements to comply with state-mandated reports.

Imbued with the commitment to communicate with students, to offer them assistance in a variety of ways that we felt sure they would appreciate and take advantage of, and to praise students for succeeding, we embarked upon our new tracking ventures.

The "Models" Aren't

The new standards of academic progress and the tracking and communicating efforts associated with them were implemented in the fall 1984 term. Over the next three years we monitored the system and experimented with several ways to best communicate with students. A student development faculty member studied and worked with students on probation as his sabbatical project. His findings, as well as the experiences of administrators, counselors, and staff working directly with students, prompted the college to simplify parts of the tracking system and to clarify or slightly revise the SOAP policies. Although still not fully satisfied that the system is ideal, we are confident that the changes made in it will smooth the implementation of standards of academic progress at the college. The tracking system is now more responsive to the diverse student population we serve, and yet we continue to maintain the academic integrity and rigor that fostered the 1984 changes.

The most important lesson we learned from the initial three years of SOAP was that our carefully formulated "models" of student progress could not begin to capture the diversity of patterns that existed and that probably no computer-based classification system could do so, because there are too many alternative explanations for the same observable behavior. Consequently, our challenge is to craft a computer-based tracking/communicating system that works accurately for most students, while at the same time incorporating opportunities for professional judgment to override or circumvent the mechanistic approach. A key to achieving this objective is to ensure that these professional judgments are supportive of the overall policy and are made and implemented consistently.

To illustrate the challenge, we present three case studies that exemplify the diverse and often ambiguous situations with which we must deal.

Case 1. Mary S. is forty-two years old, has earned a *B*+ average for the five terms she has been at the college, and has accumulated fifteen credits by taking one course a semester. In the spring term she withdraws from her course two weeks before final exams. As a result, she is placed on academic warning because she failed to meet the half-course rule. She complains that this isn't fair.

It is clear from Mary's record, however, that she was not in any real academic difficulty. From a counseling perspective the college would like to give Mary S. an opportunity to discuss the reasons for her withdrawal and, if it makes sense, to exempt her from being placed on warning.

The resolution to this challenge is to include the capability for an administrative override when a qualified student affairs staff member determines that the reasons for withdrawal are appropriate to exempt the student from being placed on an academic sanction. Examples of appropriate reasons for withdrawal are illness, sudden changes at work, or family emergencies. Inappropriate reasons are not bothering to do assigned classwork, fear of receiving a poor grade, or lack of interest in the course.

A student who believes the academic sanction is not appropriate must initiate contact with the college to seek an override. There is no way the computer can differentiate between acceptable and unacceptable reasons for failing to meet the half-course rule.

Case 2. John is a twenty-seven-year-old male student who first enrolled at the college eight years ago. He has earned only twenty-four credits. John enrolls every fall and spring but is successful only in the fall, during which he registers for three courses and successfully completes two of them. During the spring term he withdraws from his two or three courses, but he then returns in the fall to try again. His grade point average hovers just above the minimum of 2.0.

John is placed on warning at the end of each spring term because he fails to meet the half-course rule, but each fall he meets the SOAP criteria and returns to good standing. The SOAP system has not fulfilled its purpose as a safety net to identify students who seem to be in academic difficulty, because John regularly bounces between warning and good standing.

To resolve this all-too-frequent occurrence, the Office of Student Affairs obtains a list of students who fail to meet SOAP criteria in nonconsecutive terms. Personnel review the records of these students and offer assistance where deemed appropriate. The vice-president for student affairs can place a student who has failed to meet SOAP standards in nonconsecutive semesters on warning, probation, suspension, or dismissal, so long as the sanction is not more severe than that on which the student would have been placed had the failure to meet standards occurred in consecutive semesters.

Case 3. Lester is a fifty-year-old male student who decided to return to school after being laid off at his job. He enrolled in four courses, completed all of them, and earned a 3.3 grade point average. In the next term he again enrolled in four courses, but just before the term was to begin Lester was recalled to his old job. He did not inform the college that he would not be attending his classes. He had charged his tuition on his bank credit card and it became simply another addition to his credit card balance, a balance he paid in regular monthly installments. At the end of the term Lester was placed on warning because he failed to meet the half-course rule. He was angry and hurt, and argued that it wasn't the college's business whether or not he attended classes.

The issue here is, does the student have the right to simply not attend classes? At this time Oakton has not resolved this issue. On the one hand, there are those who argue that a student who never attends classes has not established an academic record and therefore cannot be in academic difficulty. They argue further that the SOAP system is designed for those in academic difficulty and therefore does not apply in a case like Lester's. On the other hand, there are those who argue that walking away from classes without formally withdrawing demonstrates academic irresponsibility and a type of behavior that should not be condoned. Therefore, proponents of this line of thinking argue that Lester should be placed on warning as a means of educating him about acceptable student behavior.

Lessons Learned

After many years of working with the SOAP policies and procedures, a number of lessons became clear.

1. A computer-based tracking system will never be able to address all the permutations of academic performance and student behavior. We need to recognize the limits of the computer program and to remember its original intent—to identify those students who might be in need of academic assistance or support. The SOAP system has proven to be a reasonable set of safety nets that catch students who exhibit defined patterns of academic behavior that we believe warrant our intervention.

2. The safety net approach will invariably include a relatively small number of students who legitimately do not belong in the net. We need to be sensitive to their appeals and to have enough personnel available with the authority and knowledge to hear these appeals and act on them. We also need to consider the number of appeals made, the time they take, and to calculate a rough cost/benefit ratio to use in determining when the volume of legitimate appeals costs more in staff time and student frustration than the benefit of identifying and offering assistance to students in academic difficulty.

3. Obtaining assistance or appealing placement on a SOAP sanction requires student initiative. The college can provide information but cannot force the passive student to act.

4. A complex system used to track transient students through their academic lives at a college needs to be reviewed and revised on a regular basis. The college must be aware of the impact of its policies and procedures on students and the difference—positive or negative—these are making in students' academic progress.

5. Faculty and staff, full- and part-time, need to be aware of the system and, in particular, the academic standards students must meet and the various stages of intervention that exist. They need to know what their responsibilities are in providing accurate, clear information, and they need to know what services are available to students and who provides them.

Perhaps the major lesson learned, and the one that we must keep in mind as we develop ever more complex and sophisticated tracking systems, is that a computer-based tracking and intervention system such as the one at Oakton is at best only a support and a supplement to the most important element of high-quality education—human involvement.

Trudy H. Bers is senior director of institutional research, curriculum, and strategic planning at Oakton College, Des Plaines, Illinois.

Alan M. Rubin is chair of the behavioral and social studies department at Oakton College, Des Plaines, Illinois.

The payoff for follow-up and student flow analysis efforts is more comprehensive and richer information about students' educational experiences and achievements.

Student Intentions, Follow-Up Studies, and Student Tracking

Michael R. Stevenson, R. Dan Walleri, Saundra M. Japely

Results from student follow-up studies can shape activities at all stages in a student tracking system. To illustrate this contention this chapter first looks at the link between follow-up results and each stage of the student flow model described by Bers in Chapter One. A case study is then presented that emphasizes the important role of student intentions in a student flow and outcomes system. A concluding section offers characteristics of a model process for developing a community college follow-up system.

Follow-Up as Part of a Student Flow Model

Awareness Stage. Generally, a person's awareness of a community college is derived from its public image, which both defines and limits the type of programs and services expected by potential students. Appropriately developed follow-up information can be used to describe what a

T. H. Bers (ed.). *Using Student Tracking Systems Effectively.*
New Directions for Community Colleges, no. 66. San Francisco: Jossey-Bass, Summer 1989.

college has done and can do for its students, and therefore to influence its public image.

The good news is that an inexpensive and quickly developed and reported follow-up study can be somewhat effective in this domain. The bad news is that a long-term commitment and significant resources are needed to develop a follow-up system that connects to other components of tracking student flow. Specifically, national or statewide cooperative efforts as well as college-based efforts are needed if student outcomes information is to influence and improve each institution's effectiveness. The Kellogg/National Center for Higher Education Management Systems (NCHEMS) Student Outcomes Project (Ewell, 1985) and the American Association of Community and Junior Colleges' (AACJC's) recent focus on student assessment and success (Kreider and Walleri, 1987; American Association of Community and Junior Colleges, 1987) are examples of appropriate cooperative efforts. Such efforts are assisting community colleges in developing both effective and appropriate student flow and outcomes systems.

Inquiry Stage. Follow-up efforts can provide insights about how students move from diffuse awareness of a community college to obtaining pertinent and sufficient information about the programs in which they enrolled. Also, follow-up efforts provide an opportunity to explore these former students' needs for further community college services. Thus follow-up efforts can be a proactive approach to student recruitment as well as a process for obtaining evaluative and outcomes information.

Entry Stage. Experiences in California (Sheldon, 1981) and in Oregon (Stevenson, 1984) have demonstrated that follow-up results describing a former student's present status are much more meaningful in the context of the student's original intentions and background at entry to the college. Long-term commitment and patience are needed to connect follow-up efforts to measures of a student's original intent and background. Collecting student intentions data, storing them, and then linking these data with follow-up results requires a systematic and comprehensive student tracking process. While this effort can be (and has been) justified on the basis of better understanding community colleges' unique stories, it requires a significant resource commitment.

Experience Stage. The impact of a community college on its students is more than the job or further education made possible or affected by the community college experience. Each student's shift in intentions, educational goal, choice of field of study, and personal development needs to be tracked and better understood.

The community college mission is to serve its clients' needs as defined by the clients rather than as primarily defined by educational professionals. This unique approach to providing higher education services—an approach that is quintessential marketing—requires a broad approach to follow-up study design. All students, not just graduates, should be asked about changes in their educational objectives, intentions, and motivations. As Alexander and Stark (1988) state:

> Traditionally, motivation, self-efficacy, involvement, and effort have been viewed as fixed attributes students bring to the educational process . . . these characteristics are subject to change (in an intended or unintended direction) as a result of the educational process . . . Although little attention has been given to these ideas, most colleges would agree, for example, that improved motivation is an outcome to be sought. While the original motivation a student brings to college is an input, a new motivational level based on educational experiences becomes an outcome the student takes to the next stage of learning [p. 14].

This commitment to measure shifts in students' intentions associated with their college experiences is a movement toward a doctor's case record approach rather than a postmortem, after the fact, traditional follow-up study approach.

Completion Stage. Follow-up activities have traditionally been focused on obtaining relevant information from students completing clearly defined programs. This nicely conforms to evaluating the effectiveness of these programs' specified objectives. However, since community colleges by their nature facilitate student-defined objectives, not only or even primarily the objectives of a program, the traditional emphasis on completers provides at best a partial assessment of perceptions and achievements of former students.

Student-defined objectives modify the traditional meaning of *completion.* For students, completion may be finishing a single course, or remediating academic basic skills deficiencies, or taking a conglomeration of courses that makes sense to the student but does not conform to a formal program or curriculum pattern. In short, this student-focused meaning of completion can be described by how well each student's unique needs (intentions) were successfully fulfilled as contrasted with how well the program's articulated purpose was fulfilled. As an aside, some students' definition of success (intentions) may not be what a college wants to support; for example, a student may wish to remain enrolled regardless of academic performance in order to qualify for financial aid or to retain eligibility for parental health insurance coverage.

A recognition of this leads to the need to follow-up on diverse groups: students who leave prior to completing their declared program of study, students who have not declared a major and who leave the college after only a few courses, course dropouts, and course registrants who do not attend their classes. When the follow-up activities are broadened to include such students, the need to compare follow-up feedback with the original intentions of each student becomes clearer. Accurately telling the community college story of many, mutually exclusive, successfully served student prototypes requires such an approach.

Case Study

Among the most difficult questions to answer about a community college are those that deal with describing student persistence, completion, and outcomes. These are difficult concepts to operationalize and describe accurately due to a large part-time student population and the diverse needs and objectives of individuals enrolling in community colleges. Problems arise from some erroneous assumptions inherent in the concepts. For example, one assumption is that all students intend to earn a degree. Another is that all students intend to earn a degree in a two- to four-year time frame. A third assumption is that students attend college during contiguous terms or drop out "for good."

It is our contention that these issues can be addressed adequately only from the students' own perspective, and not on the basis of institutional assumptions about why students enroll, or assumptions about students' intentions derived from the population of traditionally aged students at four-year colleges and universities. This case study attempts to demonstrate the value of this approach, based on the monitoring of student intentions and outcomes at Mt. Hood Community College (MHCC), a medium-size comprehensive institution located near Portland, Oregon.

The increasing national and local focus on student outcomes has centered largely on demands for accountability and concerns that the open door at many colleges had become a revolving door. MHCC attempted to work through these concerns through a campuswide group called the Student Success Task Force, which began to direct energies toward more precisely identifying student objectives and monitoring student progress toward achieving those objectives. Determining goals of entering students and adequately ascertaining goal fulfillment were two problems associated with developing an accurate measure of student success (Lenning, Beal, and Sauer, 1980).

The work of the Student Success Task Force raised several issues with regard to student flow and follow-up. For example, only fragmentary data had been available for the part-time student population. Though part-timers constitute the majority of MHCC's students, relatively little was known about them. Advisement, counseling, and data collection efforts were tailored toward full-time enrollees. Since demographic and other trends suggest that part-time attendance will account for an increasing proportion of community college enrollment, effective instructional planning and academic decision making at MHCC required a vigorous research emphasis on these students.

Still further, low graduation rates seemed to indicate the college had a high attrition rate. However, it seemed that institutional staff (and the public), not students, perceived that graduation rates should be the indicator of student success. Perhaps that standard of success was not critical to community college students, and measuring student success from the institution's perspective was inappropriate. To test these suppositions, the MHCC staff decided to collect the crucial component missing from the college's information base—student-declared intent.

Partial funding for the initial phases of the project was provided by a grant through the Kellogg/NCHEMS Student Outcomes Project (Ewell, 1983, 1985). Conceptual design and computer programming costs for the development of the intentions collection system were covered by the grant.

Influencing the MHCC project was the research of Hunter and Sheldon (1980) and Sheldon (1981) on California community college students, which demonstrated the importance of analyzing outcomes in light of student intentions. The California Statewide Longitudinal Study followed some 6,500 students for three years, from 1978 to 1981. Objectives of this study were to explain attrition, describe student self-perceptions, and determine the effect of the community college on student lives. Eighteen prototypes of California community college students based on student-described intentions and student performance were developed. No single prototype accounted for more than 14 percent of the students.

It was clear that only by directly asking each student for his/her reasons for enrolling could an accurate picture of student success be drawn. Using the identified California prototypes as a base, MHCC developed three questions on student intent—one requesting the student's occupational motive, one on educational goal, and another asking how long the student intended to remain at the college. Two background questions were also included, one on level of previous educational achievement and the other on current employment status. Table 1 details the student intentions questions asked of students at the time of registration. These questions were reviewed and updated with students upon registration in subsequent MHCC terms.

The MHCC study design attempted to integrate the findings of the California study and to replicate the results within a less ambitious and less costly research design. One of the main differences between the California study and the MHCC study is that data collection at Mt. Hood is ongoing. Rather than personally interviewing students for a one-time-only project, MHCC incorporated collection of student intentions information into ongoing institutional processes. Consequently, the collection system is an operational part of the student data base and produces useful, updated information each term.

In the fall term of 1983, in order to collect this educational intent data from every student, MHCC's admissions and records office was asked to

Table 1. Student Intentions Questions at Time of Registration at Mt. Hood Community College, Gresham, Oregon

Questions	Answers
Occupational Motive: What is your ultimate reason for attending MHCC at this time?	1. Get a job 2. Enhance current job 3. Get a better job 4. Personal enrichment 5. Explore a career direction 6. Other
Educational Goal: What are your educational aspirations?	1. Take one class 2. Take a few classes 3. Earn a two-year degree 4. Earn a one-year certificate 5. Earn a GED 6. Earn a four-year degree
Duration: How long do you intend to remain at MHCC?	1. One quarter only 2. Two quarters 3. One year 4. Two years 5. Three years 6. More than three years

solicit this information as part of its on-line registration process. The process was kept brief and concise so as to minimally impact speed of the registration process. In addition to responses to the intentions questions, demographic and academic performance data were available from student records. Also, data on student activities approximately one year after leaving MHCC were available from annual follow-up survey responses from graduates and former students. Coupling these outcomes data with the intentions data completed the circle.

Table 2 provides some indication of the degree to which student intentions were fulfilled. MHCC associate degree and certificate completion rates are based on the total population. Because intentions responses refer to outcomes after leaving the college, the follow-up results for Table 2 are based on the responses of graduates and former full-time students to a survey conducted in spring 1985.

Reviewing degree completion rates, only 21 percent of the students who indicated they planned to earn an associate degree did so within two years. The completion rate for the students with a one-year certificate intent was even lower. Those with an understanding of the complex makeup of the community college student population will not be surprised by these findings. Many students declare a degree goal because it is socially acceptable. Often their primary goal is to secure employment.

**Table 2. Fall 1983 Student Intentions by Outcomes in Spring 1985,
Mt. Hood Community College, Gresham, Oregon**

Fall 1983 Motive	Total Population (N = 9,602)	
	N	Completed (%)
Associate Degree	2951	628 (21.3)
Certificate	208	32 (15.4)
	Follow-Up Respondents (N = 428)	
	Attending Four-Year College (%)	Related to MHCC Program (%)
Bachelor's Degree	139	106 (76.3)	82 (77.4)
	Employed (%)	Related to MHCC Program (%)
Job-Related	40	29 (72.5)	21 (72.4)
Associate Degree	212	177 (83.5)	119 (67.2)
Certificate	21	16 (76.2)	9 (56.3)
Total	273	222 (81.3)	149 (67.1)

Note: The total is the number responding for the motives indicated. The table does not represent all categories reported.

Further, many students require more than two years to complete the associate degree.

Follow-up results revealed that more than 75 percent of the students who indicated an intention to earn a bachelor's degree in fall 1983 were attending a four-year institution in spring 1985. Of those who did transfer, more than 75 percent were continuing the studies originated at MHCC. Students with very low GPAs were not likely to transfer to four-year institutions. Although not reported in the table, 70 percent of those with less than a 1.99 cumulative GPA had not continued their studies. Most did find employment; however, only half indicated they were employed in a field related to their major. Of the high GPA students who continued their studies, almost all (92.5 percent) had transferred into a program related to their major at MHCC.

Of those who indicated a job-related motive, including the certificate or associate degree, more than 80 percent had secured employment. Of these, 67 percent were working in a field related to their college program. Students with high GPAs found jobs; in fact, 77 percent held a job related to their MHCC major. Overall, the follow-up results indicated a high degree of student success in terms of original student intentions.

Subsequent student follow-up surveys have found consistently high correlations between intentions and outcomes, especially with regard to transfer intentions. Information on the number of students who actually earn a four-year degree will have to wait for further analysis. For Oregon as a whole, a single preliminary study suggests that about a quarter of students beginning at a community college eventually obtain the bachelor's degree (Oregon Educational Coordinating Commission, 1987).

The MHCC intentions data offer a true picture of intentions from the student perspective. As a result, percentages of students graduating, student persistence, and student outcomes can be measured and explained with greater precision and sensitivity. This will allow the faculty and administration to respond to demands for accountability without making questionable assumptions about students' objectives and/or attrition. As George Keller (1983) notes, "Good information not only facilitates more rational decision making; it also motivates toward more strategic decision making" (p. 133).

Phases in Developing a Community College Follow-Up System

A general model for developing a student follow-up system at a community college can be outlined from the above discussion and case study of student flow and outcomes. The proposed model allows a college to clarify where it is in the development of a follow-up system, identify system issues needing attention, and promote optimal use of follow-up information.

Table 3 briefly describes the six phases of our follow-up system development model across the dimensions of institutional commitment, active involvement, and desired benefit. During the first phase (entitled WAIT), focus should be on clearly defining the audience for the data. The needs of both internal and external users should be accounted for in developing a student follow-up system. If no clear users of follow-up study results are identified readily, then the focus should be on developing the market for follow-up results (not on doing a survey). As Patton argues in his 1981 text *Creative Evaluation,* "how information is to be used should be the driving force behind how the evaluation is designed and coordinated . . . this is the personal factor—who cares about the evaluation . . . " (p. 83, 86).

The second phase (entitled PROJECT) involves the follow-up process design, especially with regard to the survey instrument(s). There is a considerable body of literature dealing with the subject of survey design (Stevenson, Walleri, and Japely, 1985). Two considerations are stressed here. First, the various user needs should be incorporated into the design. Second, it is appropriate at this stage to begin the work of connecting student follow-up to the other elements of the student flow model. An example of this was illustrated with regard to the MHCC case study on student intentions (Stevenson, 1984). When designing any survey, careful

Table 3. Follow-Up Activities Development Model

Phase	Institutional Commitment	Active Involvement	Desired Benefit
1. Wait	*I N C R* To an idea	*I N C R* Governing board and president	*I N C R* Clearer thinking
2. Project	*E A* To a survey	*E A* +Institutional researcher	*E A* Student outcomes focus
3. Program	*S I N G* To impacting academic and service improvements	*S I N G* +Academic and student service managers	*S I N G* Student outcomes-caused changes
4. Focused	*C O M P L E* To specific program, service, and support improvements	*C O S T* +Faculty and/or support staff and/or state/ federal decision makers	*I N V O L V E* Specific changes
5. System	*X I T Y* To better understanding	+Registrar and data processing	*M E N* Articulating community college stories
6. Organic	To daily collection, compilation, and use	+Students and community	*T* Student process to outcomes understanding

consideration should be given to long-range use of the results because consistent data collected from year to year renders the most useful information for trend analysis.

The third phase (entitled **PROGRAM**) involves the commitment to a consistently implemented follow-up process. This process would lead to the analysis of results and examination of trends to facilitate improving academic programs and campuswide services. For example, information on students having difficulty transferring credits to a four-year institution can result in an articulation agreement with the four-year school to simplify credit transfers.

Data on future technological advances in the work place can alert faculty to the need to rewrite curricula to address these upcoming innovations. General education requirements become higher priority when graduates, former students, and their current employers all agree reading, writing, and computing are critical skills for job success. The economic health of the local community will be revealed by data on the percentage of former students able to find full-time versus part-time employment after leaving the institution.

The power of student follow-up data can be magnified by packaging them with other program effectiveness indicators in a program assessment or strategic planning system. For example, at Mt. Hood Community

College, the follow-up data are coupled with data on program demand, cost per student, employment outlook, retention rates, and eleven other program effectiveness measures to arrive at a timely "snapshot" of each program's effectiveness. This fairly comprehensive review process offers faculty and administrators a way to review and analyze discrete program data, make comparisons and contrasts across disciplines, and assist with overall academic strategy. This review cycle feeds directly into the campuswide strategic planning and budgeting processes. Follow-up results provide some answers to the needs that Deegan, Tillery, and Associates (1985) identify: "We need to know what works and what does not, under what conditions, and at what cost" (p. 323).

The fourth phase (entitled FOCUSED) moves the institution to explore specific issues while maintaining its commitment to a consistent follow-up program. Ranking institutional issues needing attention is the key to this fourth phase. About which subgroup of students and/or specific issues does the staff need more information?

With careful planning and an eye to future needs, an inventory of desired information can be formulated and a process for compiling it can be designed. In the case of MHCC, staff chose to focus first on part-time students. As noted above, MHCC had not collected much data on part-time students, yet they comprised a larger group than full-time students. To fill this gap, MHCC research staff focused on students who had earned fifteen or more cumulative, college-transfer credits but attended only part-time (less than ten credits in any given quarter). Of the over 20,000 students attending the college in 1985–86, slightly over 3,000 students fell into this category. An examination of their expressed intentions showed that 75 percent reported the associate or four-year degree as their educational goal. These students will have to be tracked over a considerable period to make a determination of outcomes.

During the fifth phase (entitled SYSTEM) student follow-up becomes institutionalized as part of the institution's complete student flow and tracking system. Phase five is a commitment to a systematic approach to understanding the pattern of each student's progress through the college, including how intentions change as he or she moves through the college experience and beyond. Individual student success (and failure) stories provide many insights into the college experience for students. Individual student responses and response summaries by program can help advisers, counselors, admissions officers, faculty, and administrators ponder the systems in place and be more client-responsive. Staff can also attempt to disentangle the factors over which they have some control from those over which they do not, and to address the former.

The sixth and final phase (entitled ORGANIC) involves the use of student flow and outcomes analysis to improve both the teaching and learning process and the service to students. In this phase, everyone in the institution should be adept at using information to shape change. Data and information are perceived as essential for planning and implementing new or revised programs and services, and requests for data and information will undoubtedly exceed the resources of the institution to supply them.

In order to establish a model such as the one proposed in this article, strong leadership is required. To close the informational loop between student intentions and student follow-up requires an ever-increasing commitment of dollars, effort, people involvement, and data analysis. Moving from marketing potential benefits to survey design, to trends analysis, to focused analysis, to student flow analysis, and finally to organic maintenance is an arduous but rewarding task.

Conclusion

This chapter has argued that the payoff for follow-up and student-flow analysis efforts is more comprehensive and richer information about students' educational experiences and achievements. Knowing students' intentions for enrolling in college is essential, because assessments of success need to be made in the context of students' own goals and not those assumed or imposed by educators, legislators, or other participants or observers of higher education. A comprehensive student tracking system that joins data about student intentions, experiences at the college, and postcollege experiences and evaluations of the institution is a key tool to enable the institution to develop and deliver courses, programs, and services that are most effective in helping students to meet their goals and that are consistent with the mission of the institution.

References

Alexander, J. M., and Stark, J. S. "Focusing on Student Academic Outcomes: A Working Paper." School of Education, University of Michigan, 1988.

American Association of Community and Junior Colleges, "Public Policy Agenda." *AACJC Letter*, no. 273, December 29, 1987.

Deegan, W. L., Tillery, D., and Associates. *Renewing the American Community College: Priorities and Strategies for Effective Leadership*. San Francisco: Jossey-Bass, 1985.

Ewell, P. T. *Information on Student Outcomes: How to Get It and How to Use It*. Boulder, Colo.: National Center for Higher Education Management Systems, 1983.

Ewell, P. T. (ed.). *Assessing Educational Outcomes*. New Directions for Institutional Research, no. 47. San Francisco: Jossey-Bass, 1985.

Hunter, R., and Sheldon, S. *Statewide Longitudinal Study*. Parts 1-3. Woodland Hills, Calif.: Los Angeles Pierce College, 1980.

Keller, G. *Academic Strategy: The Management Revolution in American Higher Education*. Baltimore, Md.: Johns Hopkins University Press, 1983.

74

Kreider, P., and Walleri, R. "Seizing the Agenda: Institutional Effectiveness and Student Outcomes for Community Colleges." *Community College Review*, 1988, *16* (2), 44–50.

Lenning, O. T., Beal, P. E., and Sauer, K. *Retention and Attrition: Evidence for Action and Research.* Boulder, Colo.: National Center for Higher Education Management Systems, 1980.

Oregon Educational Coordinating Commission. *What Happened to the Class of '75?* Salem: Oregon Educational Coordinating Commission, 1987, p. 20.

Patton, M. Q. *Creative Evaluation.* Beverly Hills, Calif.: Sage, 1981.

Sheldon, S. M. *Statewide Longitudinal Study: 1978–1981 Final Report.* Woodland Hills, Calif.: Los Angeles Pierce College, 1981.

Stevenson, M. "Kellogg/NCHEMS Final Report on Its 3-Year Student Outcomes Information Project." Gresham, Ore.: Mt. Hood Community College, 1984.

Stevenson, M., Walleri, R. D., and Japely, S. M. "Designing Follow-Up Studies of Graduates and Former Students." In P. T. Ewell (ed.), *Assessing Educational Outcomes.* New Directions for Institutional Research, no. 47. San Francisco, Jossey-Bass, 1985.

Michael R. Stevenson is director of student information systems at the University of California, Santa Barbara.

R. Dan Walleri is director of research, planning, and administrative computing at Mt. Hood Community College, Gresham, Oregon.

Saundra M. Japely is coordinator of continuing education and professional development at Mt. Hood Community College, Gresham, Oregon.

Increased state mandates to improve higher education in Texas
led to the development of a system to track the effectiveness
of remedial education.

LONESTAR: Texas's Voluntary Tracking and Developmental Education Evaluation System

Stanley I. Adelman, Peter T. Ewell,
John R. Grable

In 1985, the Texas legislature created a Select Committee on Higher Education. The committee held open meetings across the state to gather information that could be used to formulate recommendations for improving the Texas higher education system. At one of those meetings, questions about the success of developmental education were raised, and the colleges and universities were unable to answer them. Although Texas was spending millions of dollars annually to remediate underprepared students, educators were unable to document the success of those students. Embarrassed, one educator who attended that meeting presented the problem at the next meeting of the Texas Association of Junior and Community College Instructional Administrators, the statewide association of two-year college academic vice-presidents and deans. The association created a committee to determine the state of remedial education in two-

T. H. Bers (ed.). *Using Student Tracking Systems Effectively.*
New Directions for Community Colleges, no. 66. San Francisco: Jossey-Bass, Summer 1989.

year colleges in Texas. That action was the first step on the trail to the development of the LONESTAR (*LON*gitudinal *E*valuation *S*tudent *T*racking *A*nd *R*eporting) system.

The committee first met during the summer of 1985. Three committee members invited the institutional researchers from their colleges to participate in that meeting. Under the auspices of the committee, the researchers surveyed all Texas community colleges to find out how each evaluated its remedial education program. The committee determined that little was known about the effectiveness of remedial education at most Texas colleges. As a result, the association sought the support of the Texas Public Community/Junior College Association, an association of presidents of community and junior colleges in Texas, to establish a joint committee to prepare guidelines for the evaluation of remedial programs. The committee consisted of two representatives each from the presidents' and the instructional administrators' associations, two members from the community college division of the Texas Coordinating Board for Higher Education, and the director of the remedial education program at one of the Texas community colleges. (A Texas community college institutional researcher was added later in an advisory capacity.) The coordinating board secured funds that allowed the group to contract with the National Center for Higher Education Management Systems (NCHEMS) to produce a design and a computer program to evaluate remedial education.

When the group met in December 1986, the institutional researcher and the director of the remedial program at Amarillo College presented to the group the methodology they used to evaluate the effectiveness of remedial education at their institution. The college had identified three important factors to track—student progress within the developmental program, student progress in nonremedial courses, and student progress toward degree completion among students seeking degrees. One unique facet of the approach they used was that progress was measured by the proportion of courses resulting in grades of C or higher, or in terms of the proportion of students with grade point averages of 2.0 or higher, rather than by comparing GPAs. Two comparison groups were used—students who did not need remediation and students who needed remediation and refused the service.

Following that presentation, the NCHEMS staff developed the concept of a generic tracking system—one that could be used to evaluate developmental education but that could also be used to help determine the effectiveness of nonremedial programs. The colleges, now also facing new institutional effectiveness criteria enacted by the Southern Association of Colleges and Schools (SACS), enthusiastically supported the broad perspective of the NCHEMS proposal.

Design

By the end of that meeting, the structure of what was to become known as LONESTAR was clear. It was to be a set of computer files and reports, based on a cohort concept, that could be used to track student performance at an institution from the time the student first enrolled at the college. Elements needed to determine remedial program effectiveness would be particularly emphasized.

By the LONESTAR definition, a cohort contains three types of students. Included are (1) all credit students who are new to the college during a particular term, (2) credit students who had been away from the college for more than six years, and (3) first-time noncredit students in GED, English as a second language, and other programs consisting of more than 360 contact hours. The performance of each cohort was to be tracked for six years.

Each participating college would be expected to supply LONESTAR with the items needed by the system, but the items would have to match LONESTAR definitions. Each institution was on its own in this phase. Once this data gathering was complete, however, LONESTAR software would be designed in common to accomplish the design goals.

After examining a number of alternatives, NCHEMS recommended that LONESTAR be written in SPSS (Statistical Package for the Social Sciences). SPSS had three important advantages. First, it had sufficient data base capabilities to handle needed file manipulations. Second, it had a fine report generator and an abundance of useful statistical procedures. Third, it ran on virtually all brands of mainframe computers, and it had a parallel package for microcomputers. This was especially important because of the diversity of computing installations in Texas community colleges.

Data Elements

During the next five months, the data elements and reports that comprise the LONESTAR system were defined by the group with help from NCHEMS. Where one existed, a Texas definition structure was used for each element. If an element did not have a Texas definition, the group turned to any recognized national definition. In those instances where elements had neither Texas nor national definitions, NCHEMS or the group or both created the definitions.

Three types of elements were included in the system—fixed elements collected at college admission, semi-fixed items that are to be updated one time, and term performance elements.

The fixed elements are arranged as follows in six files:

- Basic demographic information: gender, date of birth, and ethnic identification
- Optional demographic information: level of parents' education, marital status, and number of dependents
- Educational background information: high school performance and remediation status
- Optional educational background information: high school rank and remedial test scores
- First-term enrollment status information: some financial aid information, location and time of attendance, major, and so on
- Optional enrollment status information: whether financial aid is need-based.

The semi-fixed items are included in a single file called remediation performance. Included in this file are performance in first college-level English and math courses.

Term performance items are contained in three files:

- Beginning-of-term update information: hours attempted and remediation attempted
- End-of-term update information: hours completed, grade point averages and remediation completed
- Optional tracking information: honor points and performance on retakes of remediation placement tests.

For more information about the data elements see Ewell, Parker, and Jones (1988).

LONESTAR labels each item as required or optional. The word *required* has proved an unfortunate choice. With the involvement of the Texas Higher Education Coordinating Board, this wording implied that all community colleges would have to collect and track such items. In LONESTAR *required* means an element will appear in a standard report. The reports would still run without those elements, but missing required elements would produce rows of zeros or blanks on the standard reports. It was never intended that required elements must be collected by every participating institution. The misunderstanding became even more pronounced in late summer 1987, when the Texas legislature passed House Bill 2182 and Senate Bill 543. These bills, among other things, required colleges to collect information to evaluate remedial education (and other topics) for the first time. These two legislative acts did mandate collection and tracking of certain information. As of May 1988, colleges can use LONESTAR to meet these reporting requirements, but no school is required to participate in LONESTAR to do so.

Reports

The LONESTAR system contains nine standard reports. Each report can be run for any cohort (or any subset of any cohort) for up to nineteen terms of performance. Each report has columns indicating performance and rows indicating student background factors.

There are two institutional progress reports, one with raw numbers and one with percents indicating factors such as current enrollment and graduation. An institutional performance report shows items like average GPA and terms needed to graduate.

There are three institutional remediation reports. The first covers initial placement test performance and whether, if needed, remediation is complete. The third shows when remediation was completed, performance in nonremedial areas, and number graduated. The second is slightly different. Its rows show remediation need rather than background factors. Its columns, like those in remediation report three, contain time needed to complete remediation, performance in nonremedial courses, and graduation results.

The last three reports, a state-level progress report and two state-level remediation reports, are extracts of the institution-level reports. They were "best guesses" of what the state might require as a result of pending legislation when the reports were written. These reports may well change as the state further defines reporting requirements now that House Bill 2182 and Senate Bill 543 are law.

Implementation

By the beginning of June 1987, eight community colleges, one technical institute, and one university had agreed to act as pilot institutions for the project. Some schools used the mainframe version of LONESTAR; others used the microcomputer version. The most difficult task, however, for each institution was getting the data into the format required by LONESTAR.

Overall, institutions with locally developed registration systems had fewer problems than did schools with proprietary registration systems as they incorporated new items and secured, recoded, and organized existing items for LONESTAR. It quickly became apparent that some proprietary systems facilitate this kind of data extraction, and others virtually prohibit it without expensive new programming.

Some institutions attempted to implement only the required elements of LONESTAR. Others tried to implement virtually the entire system. The most difficult required item to secure was a complex element that represented various categories of financial aid status. Some schools could not secure the data at all; others could only indicate whether a student had received financial aid. Only one institution could indicate all five of the codes suggested by NCHEMS.

Part of the pilot year funds were dedicated to on-site campus visits by NCHEMS. These visits were extremely helpful, not only in getting the

SPSS and LONESTAR software up and running but also in providing suggestions for data extraction.

In April 1988, all other state institutions interested in using LONE-STAR met in Austin. Approximately fifty-five additional institutions agreed to participate. Since funds would not be available to allow on-site NCHEMS visits for the new institutions, two techniques were instituted to provide needed support. First, each pilot institution would act as a consultant to the new participants in its geographic area. Second, training in SPSS would be provided at LONESTAR meetings throughout the 1988–89 fiscal year. The training would cover both generic SPSS operations and a detailed presentation of the LONESTAR application and additional local use of the LONESTAR files.

Institutional Benefits from LONESTAR

Most pilot institutions have realized two benefits from LONESTAR. For the first time, they now have an analysis tool to help them evaluate the effectiveness of their remedial education program. Second, they now have a tool that will help them demonstrate institutional effectiveness. These, of course, were the design goals for LONESTAR. What benefit would accrue to an institution that was prepared to both evaluate its remedial program and longitudinally track its students? One such institution, Amarillo College, participated in the pilot version.

At Amarillo it was found that, for the first time, both the remedial information and the tracking information could be integrated. For the first time six-year performance of remedial performance would be available by major. LONESTAR also provided a much more accurate record of the timing of intervention strategies. In addition, a wealth of background factors and term-to-term performance factors were now available in a tracking system.

Beyond that, the college now had a system that was instantly available for important ad hoc analyses. The standard LONESTAR reports provide useful information, but imagine the additional analysis possible in a system containing fifty-nine background items and twenty-eight performance variables repeated in each of the nineteen terms for which LONE-STAR was designed. Furthermore, each cohort file is instantly available, and it never has to be recreated. If a college is interested, for example, in whether hours employed is related to academic performance—while controlling for major, remediation needs, and hours enrolled—LONESTAR provides the files and the SPSS training to make such an analysis simple. The researcher merely needs to decide whether to do the analysis at the end of the first term, the second term, the tenth term, or the nineteenth term. Of course, the analysis could also be done at the end of each term to determine whether persistence was an important factor.

LONESTAR was designed primarily for institutions that could not afford to support an institutional research function. The standard reports provide any institution with valuable information about the nature and performance of its students. Ultimately, however, because of the ease of ad hoc analyses, the major benefit of LONESTAR may well be a widespread increased institutional focus on student outcomes.

References

Ewell, P. T., Parker, R., and Jones, D. P. *Establishing a Longitudinal Student Tracking System.* Boulder, Colo.: National Center for Higher Education Management Systems, 1988.

Stanley I. Adelman is data base coordinator and institutional researcher at Amarillo College, Amarillo, Texas.

Peter T. Ewell is senior associate at the National Center for Higher Education Management Systems in Boulder, Colorado.

John R. Grable is president of Brazosport College in Lake Jackson, Texas.

This chapter explores the roles the computer can play in the student tracking process.

Computers and Student Flow/Tracking Systems

Judith W. Leslie

Should the computer have a role in the play *Student Tracking in Community Colleges?* If the casting director were someone engaged in the field of information technology, he/she would probably say "a leading role." But what if the director were a faculty member, one who had never put his/her fingers on a keyboard and shied away from viewing information on a computer screen? He/she may think the computer should not have a role in this intensely human-to-human interactive play; at best, the computer may be viewed as merely backstage, or as a prop to feature the major performers.

This chapter will present information about what roles the computer is capable of playing, illustrate some of these roles in operation at a single institution, and address issues raised by the infusion of technology into the student tracking process in community colleges. After reading this chapter, you will have a basis for answering the question "What role can the computer perform in my institution's student tracking play?"

This chapter is divided into three major sections. The first section presents what roles the computer has already performed, using the opening analogy of the theater. While recognizing that this approach may lack the sophistication that more computer-knowledgeable readers expect, it does present the information in nontechnical terms to communicate

T. H. Bers (ed.). *Using Student Tracking Systems Effectively.*
New Directions for Community Colleges, no. 66. San Francisco: Jossey-Bass, Summer 1989.

with the broad audience consisting of all those persons involved in the student tracking process within an institution. Five "plays," or student tracking processes, are discussed: (1) admissions, (2) assessment, (3) registration, (4) advising and counseling, and (5) follow-up.

The second section of this chapter describes how the computer is used to track students in the Maricopa County Community College District, which is a multicollege district comprised of seven colleges and two centers, serving 80,000 students in the Phoenix, Arizona, metropolitan area. Although this represents a large total institution, the size of the individual colleges within the district ranges from 2,200 students at South Mountain Community College, to 8,000 at Scottsdale, to 17,000 at Mesa Community College. Thus, the description can have applicability to readers from small, medium, or large institutions. Like many other institutions, the Maricopa District has made considerable progress in automating the student tracking process in some areas, yet still needs to do more in other areas. And, perhaps like you, Maricopa continues to explore what is the proper balance between automation and personalized contact.

The third and concluding section of this chapter pertains to issues related to the infusion of technology into the student tracking process. Some are specific to Maricopa; however, most pertain to community colleges in general. The observations made are intended to highlight the advantages and disadvantages of using technology to track students.

Tell Me, What Previous Parts Have You Performed?

As noted above, this section uses the opening analogy of a theater context. The computer is used in the first person. The students are the audience; the faculty, staff, and administration (along with the computer) are the actors; the institution is the theater; and the student tracking process is the play. Let's listen now to the computer discuss what roles it has performed in student tracking plays.

Background. In my younger days, the parts I performed were primarily related to census plays—you know, like counting how many people lived in a city, a state, a country. That gave some agents the idea that I could be used in college and university plays where they needed to count students. I had stiff competition for the part, though, since people with many years of experience counted students using paper and pencil. Some of the better ones used adding machines. The toughest ones to compete against were those "warm, fuzzy" faculty who were interested in the students and advised them in a caring way. I still have trouble getting a part today when I have to compete with them. However, as my talents have improved, I have been getting better parts.

I am known to play three characters: a mainframe (I portray a big number cruncher, who lives in a specially equipped room), a minicomputer (this character is rather schizophrenic; sometimes I seem like the mainframe and other times like the microcomputer), and a microcomputer (I look small when I play this character, but increasingly I have the same capabilities as the minicomputer character while maintaining direct contact with the audience and other actors and performing in a colorful way).

I also have some ancillary characters that I portray called related communications technologies such as the phone and scanning equipment. In recent years, I've noticed that varying aspects of the characters I play all seem to be interrelating with each other. Now let me tell you about the type of plays in which I have performed a role.

Student Admissions. These plays are intended to give both the actors and audience the information they need to complete the admissions process. For example, I can provide the actors with a report on applicant profiles or, if they are interested, comparative enrollment reports. I can provide the audience with information about specific programs, services, and requirements and inform them of their current status in the admissions process.

I have been in more admissions plays in universities, four-year colleges, and private two-year colleges than I have been in community colleges. Probably because most community colleges now realize that information related to community college admissions processes can be an important resource for recruiting, I will be appearing in more community college theaters.

Assessment. These plays are intended to gather information predictive of student success. I can help the audience in decision making by giving them information as to what courses should be taken at what point based upon their abilities. I can provide the actors with organized information to predict a student's ability to succeed in a given program, patterns of enrollment, student characteristics and needs, and information regarding nonregistrants and dropouts.

There haven't been too many of these plays in community colleges. In recent years, however, the call for accountability and quality has led to changes in admissions policies. Some community colleges now have mandatory assessment testing and some have mandatory placement based upon the test results. As these policies spread to more community colleges, they will realize that I can play a key role. I have been hired by some agencies to play the role for community colleges, for example, the American College Testing Program and the Educational Testing Service.

Student Registration. These are the plays that I have been doing for the longest period of time. Registration plays are the process used to enter the student into a course(s) that leads to achievement of an educational goal. For example, I can provide a conflict-free schedule of classes;

schedule equitably for both students and faculty; and integrate other features such as library encumbrances, tuition and fee assessments, and class lists for instructors. The audience can be composed of both credit and noncredit students, although the former audience is more common. The registration play generally includes five scenes: advance registration, open registration, late registration, program adjustment/drop and add, and open entry/open exit registration.

I don't have too much difficulty backstage in the registration plays, although when we get a full house, I can be so frightened that not a word comes out: They say I've "crashed." And when I have a new wardrobe (software), I sometimes have to alter it, even during registration. I primarily use my mainframe and minicomputer characters since these plays are typically more than my microcomputer character can portray. My cousin, the phone, is playing an increasingly important role in these plays, allowing the audience to enjoy the play right at home, work, or a shopping mall. In a few registration plays, my cousin and I are the only actors since I can now generate a voice response when a student uses a phone to register. Now that's center stage!

Advising and Counseling. These plays are intended to provide those services and information that will support the students in achieving their educational goals. They are offered prior to enrollment, most heavily during registration, and on a continuous basis throughout the students' educational experience. My parts include information on course advisement, program planning, and student monitoring and intervention. Specific plays that have been produced to illustrate these functions are degree audit and academic alert systems.

A degree audit play determines if students are satisfactorily completing a degree or certificate. These plays inform students of courses that are needed to receive an award (degree or certificate), notify students when they are enrolled automatically for graduation, monitor special enrollment status, and provide a procedure for equating incoming transfer courses.

In an academic alert play, students are informed of within-term progress and attendance in all courses. Students can be referred to specific help available, if necessary, and students are notified of their standing measured against the college's standards of academic progress at the end of term. It also can provide statistical information about within-term progress of students as compared to end-of-term progress after intervention strategies are used. One of the best of these plays is at Miami-Dade Community College.

There also are other types of plays such as orientation to the campus, transfer seminars, financial aid, referral to appropriate services, and career exploration.

Whenever I get into these plays, however, I have a difficult time carrying out my role as successfully as I would like to and am capable of doing. For one thing, I have to deal with so many actors: admissions office staff, faculty advisers, counselors, and even volunteers. And from their vantage point, these actors generally have been successful in the past without my backstage support. Some, however, recognize the value of the information I can provide them so that they can better relate to the audience.

I think these plays have been produced only recently because they can be very complex, particularly in community colleges where there are numerous occupational and transfer programs, students' patterns of attendance are irregular, and their educational goals are varied. In fact, the majority of community college students are not degree-seeking. A degree audit system, therefore, must be expanded to encompass enough information to serve as a system that monitors academic progress in achieving educational goals. Although I strongly prefer to play my mainframe and minicomputer characters in these plays, there are some advising and counseling plays in which I can play my microcomputer computer character—for example, information on orienting a student to campus.

Student Follow-Up

These plays can be similar in script and run concurrently with a number of the other plays already described, especially the advising and counseling plays. There are a number of different types: transfer systems, job placement systems, alumni systems, foundation systems, and follow-up studies. They are intended to assist students in furthering their career/educational goals and to assist the institution in evaluating its effectiveness and developing/maintaining a continuing basis of public support. To illustrate these purposes, several plays are described.

A transfer play provides program transfer information to students by major for typical transfer institutions and informs students when enrolled in a course that is not required for the degree and/or not required as part of a major at the institution where they plan to transfer. A job placement play lists jobs and students are informed of openings and given referrals. The third type of play is external follow-up. These have a mechanism (usually a survey) to determine the progress/status of students who have met stated goals after they have left the institution; inquiries are made to former students and their employers or their transfer institutions regarding program strengths, weaknesses, and adequacy of preparation for employment or transfer. Pima Community College has particularly good job placement and follow-up plays.

I haven't had too many parts in these plays except as produced by universities and four-year colleges where they have alumni programs. The roles that I have performed in student follow-up plays in community colleges have been primarily as a record keeper for alumni, sometimes using only my microcomputer character. As the play critics call for better plays, however, I expect that my role will increase. I will have to work with some of my new friends and relatives, communications technologies, to do so. They can provide networking from institution to institution for electronic transfer of data; they can scan survey results into me, phone students at home/work to survey them, and maintain continuous contact with students by giving them access to information from the institution through a network that they can dial into from home or work.

That gives you some idea of my qualifications to perform a role in your play. You may ask for a current reference. However, to see just how well I've performed and how extensively, let's turn now to one of my current community college plays.

Maricopa Community Colleges Student Tracking Play

Background. The tracking of students at the Maricopa Community Colleges probably has paralleled the history of most institutions: lots of file cabinets stuffed with student records in the offices of registrars and financial aid directors, and in the business office. Faculty drawers and bookcases included old frayed catalogues, some years missing, others with notes stuffed in them. Little was known about graduates or students who periodically took courses.

In the sixties, however, an automated batch record-keeping system, designed in-house, became available. The hard copies still persisted, however, as a supplement to or duplicate for automated records. Then came a year of evaluation, 1982, a time to step back in order to look ahead. As a result of these extensive evaluation and organizational changes, in 1982–83 the Maricopa District decided upon purchasing a student information system from Information Associates, along with financial records, human resources, and alumni development systems. Digital Equipment was selected as the hardware vendor, and computer equipment was decentralized to parallel the mode of governance of the district.

Admissions Plays. Many community colleges do not have automated admissions systems. This was true about Maricopa until June 1988, when a new version of their student information system was installed. Now, those features appropriate to an open admissions institution are available, such as statistics about students who are interested in attending, enrollee versus nonenrollee characteristics, and information about students that will be a basis for individualized follow-up, including a computer-generated letter.

Assessment Play. The Maricopa District implemented a mandatory assessment testing process beginning in 1986–87. They used the American College Testing program ASSET. Tests are scored by ACT, and statistical reports are available on the performance of students. These test results will be incorporated into the Monitoring Academic Performance System (MAPS) so that an instructor, adviser, or student may view his/her test scores. This play is still relatively new, however, and will need further rehearsal.

Registration Play. The Student Information System (SIS) now serves approximately 80,000 credit students who attend the Maricopa Community Colleges. It is an on-line system so that students are expeditiously processed. Two of the colleges use phone registration (perception technology) to supplement the regular registration process. The SIS has the following specific applications: student records, billing and receivables, and financial aid.

Advising and Counseling Play. In cooperation with Information Associates, the Maricopa Community Colleges developed a degree audit system. It is a comprehensive student tracking system called MAPS. The system was installed in September 1987 and is being implemented throughout the district in varying stages depending upon the college's readiness and training schedule.

The system has three components. The first is program (catalogue) construction, which is used to build the computerized catalogue descriptions of programs, certificates, and degree requirements. These programs are then matched against students' academic programs to determine if they have met the requirements: This is the audit, the second component of the system. It includes student-specific programs; supports trial audits; handles substitutions, waivers, and exemptions; and provides for adviser comments and graduation check-out process. The system has the capability to include financial and academic holds. Academic statistics, test scores, and a minitranscript also are available. A "polling" feature is available so that an adviser can determine if students have taken course work at one of the other colleges in the district. To assist users, there are on-line help and documentation and audits that can be made available through on-line viewing or batch processing.

The third component is reporting, which includes the audit reports and additional reports used to help maintain the system. These lists are convenient formats for viewing data that are too extensive for screen displays or only required as reference material. Other uses of these reports include curriculum management, which will provide information on how courses and programs are being used within the institution.

There is a separate system called a guidance information system, which is used for advising students prior to, during, or when transferring. It provides information to prospective and current students regarding other institutions' programs and career information on a state, regional, and national level. A number of high schools also use the system.

To utilize the information available from these systems/applications for planning and decision making, a decision support system, developed by Information Associates, is being tested at the Maricopa Community Colleges. This system accesses summarized, longitudinal information from the SIS and MAPS and presents it in graphic form.

Student Follow-Up Plays. These plays are just opening at the Maricopa Community Colleges. They have an alumni development system that has been installed, and in 1988, it was extended to all the colleges as they initiated alumni activities and fundraising campaigns. Other follow-up that has recently been initiated includes the exchange of information with Arizona State University regarding the numbers of transfers and co-enrolled students. Other student tracking systems/applications include an automated job placement system that lists jobs from Phoenix employers and students who are interested in either part- or full-time employment. In addition, the job placement system will begin to yield summarized information on the numbers of students placed in jobs and other follow-up information.

Summary. I think you can see that I have been extensively involved in Maricopa plays. Much of the time I am backstage; however, in the registration process, I play one of the leading roles at some colleges. The MAPS, when fully implemented, will show just how good I can be in a student tracking play. The Maricopa Community Colleges have not yet fully used me in their student follow-up plays, although I am getting increasingly larger parts. And I need to work with some of my cousins more: phone, scanning, interactive video, laser storage technology, and color graphics. Since the chancellor, Paul Elsner, believes in "one-stop student services," I know that I have the necessary talents to play a lead role in Maricopa student tracking plays.

What Do the Critics Say?

Like other actors, I eagerly and anxiously await the critics' analysis and commentary. When they critique my plays, they tend to analyze the following aspects: (1) performance (How good was I?), (2) appropriateness (Was I right for the part?), (3) cost (What salary did I command?), (4) my interactions with other actors (How did I fit in the play?), and (5) my potential for future engagements (Will I ever make it to Broadway?). Let's read what they have to say about me.

Performance. "The computer is one of the best performers to date, especially in student registration plays," said one critic.

"You can never rely on the computer to deliver a consistent performance, especially when there is a full house," said another, less complimentary critic.

With such varying opinions as to my performance, what are you to conclude? Well, let's examine my capabilities in more detail. My mainframe character has the capability to collect, store, manipulate, and disseminate large quantities of information and do so more quickly and accurately than can other actors. When there are student tracking functions that need this capability, I am your best choice. I can also perform sophisticated calculations better than most other actors. Advising plays such as degree audit or academic alert especially need me to perform a role. And I can extract and tailor information to an individual student. So, if you are interested in having quantifiable information about a specific student, I excel in those plays.

I haven't performed well in plays when I have been tired (poorly maintained), overworked (insufficient memory or storage to handle the processing or storage of information), have an out-of-date wardrobe (have not kept up with industry software standards), and have inadequate accommodations (proper cooling, correct and up-to-date networking). To make sure that these conditions are not present, I need a good manager: one who has experience with computers, one who has the support of the administration, and one who employs and manages a good staff.

Appropriateness. "The computer has more of the talents needed in a student tracking play than any other actor to date." This critic, I like.

"Nothing can substitute for personal attention an adviser can give to an individual student in a face-to-face meeting in a comfortable office, especially something as impersonal as a computer." Oh, that one is harsh!

This is one of the heavily debated issues regarding student tracking plays. To respond, I can only answer that I want a part in those plays for which I am best suited. When the information resource is needed, I should be there. When understanding, support, and empathy are appropriate, the other actors should play the leading role.

Some of my characters are more appropriate to certain plays than are others. For example, my mainframe character is most appropriate for a registration play; my minicomputer character is effective in plays of moderate scope and length such as a student orientation system; my microcomputer character can be very good for use by advisers to build a specialized data base at their work station regarding specific students. All of these characters can be networked (using various communication technologies such as microwave, fiber optics, cabling) into a single performer and utilized in some aspect of nearly all student tracking plays.

Cost. "The declining salary demands of the computer have made it one of the most sought-after actors in the field," I read in one newspaper.

"The computer requires an inexhaustible source of income. It is never satisfied. How can one performer demand so much?" Whew, that one is the worst comment yet!

In support of the first critic, there are numerous articles citing the decreasing cost of technology. Hardware, in particular, has declined dramatically in cost. However, as I perform in plays, more people want me and new plays are developed for me. And as I develop additional characters (hardware), I have new plays for which I am appropriate. My success is killing me! However, even though the cost for my many performances in many plays has resulted in an increase in theater costs overall, the audience is getting more for its money on a cost-per-ticket basis.

Where I will admit to being costly is in my wardrobe—software. The cost of a wardrobe has increased dramatically due to the cost of the tailors (programmers, analysts). While most theaters used to make the wardrobes for their performers, many now contract out to companies who specialize in wardrobe design and manufacture (software vendors). They are noted to have a greater level of expertise than is frequently the case in a single theater's tailors and produce a wardrobe much more quickly than can a single theater.

The Maricopa theater purchased software from a vendor and then also jointly designed and manufactured software with the vendor. This combination worked exceedingly well. They had the vendor's resources and expertise combined with the local tailors' understanding of the environment in which it should fit, as well as expertise to compliment that of the vendor.

Interactions with Other Actors. "The other actors in the play felt that they performed their best when the computer was in the same play." Nice compliment.

"The computer just doesn't fit in these plays. Its character is too complex, it is impersonal, and most of the other actors just can't take the time that seems to be required to get to know the computer. Stick to the caring, spontaneous, and creative actors!" How do I handle that comment?

If I am recognized as an information resource that is easy to access, utilize, and maintain, I can work well with the other actors. It is when my wardrobe (software) doesn't fit the scenes that I have the most difficulty. The other actors don't get near me, and the audience never even sees me perform. I am finding new ways of getting to know the actors: self-paced tutorials, on-line help and documentation, easy-to-use software that includes a mouse device to move about the screen rather than a keyboard, the use of pictures and graphs, and continual training support. If my wardrobe is right and the actors can spend time learning about me, together we can give a stunning performance.

Potential for Future Engagements. "Unless the computer gets its act together by giving a consistently good performance at a reasonable cost and gets along well with the other actors, it is doomed to go the way of other shooting starlets." Oh my, I thought I had my act together. Let's read another critic's opinion.

"The potential to deliver effective, individualized, and comprehensive student tracking plays has never been greater, given the current and future talents of the computer. The Broadway play of the future will give the computer top billing." That's more like it.

But what will it take to reach Broadway? A number of key conditions are necessary. First, there must be a commitment by the theater management to include the computer in all of its student tracking plays. Without this commitment, the computer will not have the support of its fellow actors and will not have an appropriate wardrobe. Its characters will be out of date, and its performance will never reach its full potential. The theater management that does make a commitment, however, will have better plays and probably attract a growing audience who will learn and enjoy the play more than they do at other theaters lacking the commitment.

A second important condition is that the management must cast the computer in the most appropriate roles. The computer must be recognized as a theater resource, and consequently, must be planned, managed, and evaluated as are other resources such as personnel, capital, and financial resources. Without this stewardship, the computer could be relegated to being a prop.

A third condition necessary to reach Broadway is that the other actors must get to know the computer. This will entail a commitment of their time and should include assistance from those who have knowledge of the computer. When the other actors get to know the computer, they will increasingly include it in all scenes of the plays. Management and the other actors should carefully select which wardrobe (software) best fits the play through evaluation, reference checking, and cost analysis.

Let us assume that these conditions were present. Then what would a future Broadway play, starring the computer, be like? The title of the play would be something like *Computers and Communication Technologies: The Cutting Edge of Student Success*. Let's sit through Act One.

Scene One: A thirty-five-year-old student named Juan is sitting down at a microcomputer in his bedroom. He clicks his fingers and the computer turns on and a screen full of icons (miniature pictures/symbols) appears. He touches the icon that represents colleges and universities. The screen then shows five smaller screens simultaneously, depicting pictures of different institutions, including the local community college, to which he points. A picture then appears that is similar to your television screen, and a woman welcomes Juan to the institution and asks what he would like to know about the college. A menu comes up at the side with a number of different categories. Juan points to the category titled Financial Aid. He is asked a series of questions by the woman on the screen, which he answers. Some music plays, and then a profile of financial eligibility appears on the screen. He states that he would like to see how the profile would change if he got a second job at minimum wage. When he sees the results, Juan decides he won't work at a second job. Juan points to the bottom of the screen to return to the initial menu.

Scene Two: Juan goes on to select the box that symbolizes Other Student References. He hears a number being dialed, and then a student's face appears on the screen. After they have talked about the institution, Juan decides to see how his old high school course work and some classes at another college would fit with the institution's requirements for selected programs. He uses the menu to request that his high school and other college transcripts be matched with the preengineering program at the college. A profile appears that outlines what courses he would need to take, in which sequence and in what mode, and which would include interactive video courses that he could take while at home. The woman's face appears again and asks Juan if he would like to discuss what his potential would be to succeed in that program of study and that career, including transferring to a university. Juan says, "Only if it doesn't hurt."

Scene Three: A series of multiple screens pass by Juan; some are text and some are images. He points or moves a mouse on a pad to indicate an answer, and some he responds to orally. When finished, a colorful graph appears that predicts Juan's success in the program he has selected. Another graph appears that compares Juan's personality and interests to those professionals who are working in the field he has selected. Juan notes that his chances for success in the course work look good but that his personality is quite different than that of those already in the field. He points to the Help icon. A man's face appears; his name is Diego. Juan discusses with him what problems he might encounter in the field, given his personality differences from those of professionals in the field. After a lengthy discussion, Juan feels much better about his choice and makes the determination to enroll in the college and pursue his educational and career goals.

And that concludes Act One. If this play interests you, why not start writing your own? Solicit the support of your theater management, including the necessary resources; select your computer; evaluate and obtain or design your own wardrobe; familiarize the other actors with the computer; and get ready to open your Student Tracking Play.

Judith W. Leslie, previously director of computer services at the Maricopa Community College District in Phoenix, Arizona, is vice-president for information management for Information Associations in Atlanta, Georgia.

In addition to exploring the trends and issues in the development of student tracking systems, this chapter's references provide a good source for further research and study.

Trends and Issues: Student Tracking Systems at Community Colleges

Jim Palmer

Student tracking systems are part of the response to demands that institutional accountability be grounded on the assessment of student progress and outcomes. As longitudinal data bases that document the educational progress of student cohorts on a term-to-term basis, tracking systems change the focus of institutional research from such questions as "How many students are enrolled?" or "What is the current expenditure per student?" to more telling questions, such as "What percent of our students meet their educational goals?" or "Do remedial programs successfully prepare students for college-level work?" The ability of colleges to make this change in research emphasis will in large part determine whether student outcomes assessment, however widely accepted in theory, becomes a permanent fixture in practice.

This change in research orientation will not be easy. Long accustomed to the demands of state and federal data collection agencies that focus on cross-sectional data (such as enrollment or expenditures), community colleges have relatively little experience conducting longitudinal analyses of student flow and outcomes. Furthermore, many community colleges have no institutional research office, and when such offices are

T. H. Bers (ed.). *Using Student Tracking Systems Effectively.*
New Directions for Community Colleges, no. 66. San Francisco: Jossey-Bass, Summer 1989.

in place, they are often staffed by one or two persons. In a national survey of a sample of community colleges, the National Council for Research and Planning (1987) determined that 43 percent had no centralized institutional research office. The American Association of Community and Junior Colleges' (AACJC's) annual fall surveys of the nation's community colleges yield less encouraging data; less than 50 percent of the colleges indicate that they have a staff person whose formal responsibilities include institutional research and planning. There is a real danger that demands for the documentation of institutional effectiveness through the assessment of student outcomes threaten to outstrip the research capacity of many community colleges.

The development of student tracking systems, then, is not simply a matter of data processing expertise. More fundamental issues and questions need to be addressed. One issue deals with the way student data are collected and archived at community colleges: How can college data collection activities be modified to produce longitudinal, term-by-term assessments of student progress? The second issue focuses on what data are to be collected: How can researchers draw a practical balance between all that we would like to know about our students and the limited capacity of most institutional research offices? A third issue involves student follow-up: How can student tracking systems incorporate indicators of student educational or vocational progress after they leave the community college? A final issue deals with the use of information: How will the data collected in a student tracking system be used in institutional planning and improvement? Responses to each of these questions will affect the degree to which student tracking systems are successfully implemented.

College Data Collection Effort

While colleges routinely collect data on their students, most of this data collection activity does not inform policymakers about student flow and progress. Data from student applications, registration forms, transcripts, follow-up studies, and other sources are collected in separate offices and for different purposes. Some colleges pull these data together on occasion to complete retrospective analyses of the enrollment and retention patterns of student cohorts who enrolled at some point in the past. (For examples, see Doan and others, 1986; Lucas, 1986; and McConochie, 1983.) Those building student tracking systems, on the other hand, make the development of longitudinal cohort files a part of the college's regular data collection operation, ensuring that measures of student progress are updated on a term-by-term basis. Examples include the LONESTAR system developed for the Texas community colleges (Ewell, Parker, and Jones, 1988; see Chapter Nine of this volume) and the student tracking system developed at Arapahoe Community College in Colorado (described in Chapter Four of this volume).

At a minimum, then, the creation of a student tracking system requires that colleges reorganize the data already in hand. As the National Center for Higher Education Management Systems (NCHEMS) stresses in its description of the LONESTAR system: "The decision to construct a system of this kind recognizes that much of the data required to answer questions of institutional effectiveness already reside in institutional data files. The major task is to organize it in ways that will allow for appropriate analysis and reporting" (Ewell, Parker, and Jones, 1988, p. 1). This requires the skills of an individual who knows where various student data reside at the college, who has the ability to extract pertinent data from these files, and who can recode and combine these data into cohort files.

Existent data sets on campus, however, often provide an insufficient base for outcomes assessment, and the college's data collection effort has to be enlarged or modified. For example, many colleges do not routinely require entering students to specify their educational goals, thus limiting the ability of institutional researchers to correlate student outcomes with student objectives. In these cases, researchers starting a tracking system may request that students be asked about their goals during the registration process. This may be opposed by admissions officials who want to make registration as short and convenient for students as possible. But if the tracking system is to be driven by research questions, rather than by the data that happen to be available, the entire data collection effort of the college may have to be reassessed and brought into the service of the student tracking effort.

In short, tracking systems cannot be fully developed out of the institutional researcher's hip pocket. As Ewell (1987) points out, outcomes assessment requires "visible, integrated, ongoing efforts governed by established policy and involving regular (and generally centralized) data collection and analysis" (p. 10). While individual campus offices will continue to collect data for their own purposes, there will have to be some coordination so that data are collected with an eye toward increasing available information about students and their educational progress.

What Data Should Be Collected?

Part of this coordination will of necessity involve selecting a small number of data elements from the almost infinite number of variables that might potentially be included in the student tracking system (Ewell, Parker, and Jones, 1988). While it is tempting to tack onto the tracking system multiple measures of student persistence and outcomes, the costs of data entry, processing, and analysis dictate that the size of the tracking system's data base be limited. Without such limitations, tracking systems and the outcomes assessment programs they serve may die of their own weight. On a national level, the abandoned Vocational Education Data System (VEDS) is a case in point. Started in the mid-1970s to assess the student outcomes associated with programs funded by the federal vocational education act, VEDS was designed to gather data on the many subpopulations targeted for special attention by the legislation, including women, minorities, and the handicapped. In addition, VEDS called on states to report vocational education data in numerous program categories. The intent was noble, but the results were disastrous, demonstrating that policymakers do not always understand the link between the information they want and the research effort required to generate that information. Barnes (1984) explains:

> If participation in vocational education programs is relevant for manpower planning, we may want to distinguish 116 varieties of target occupations, but if vocational education is also good for sex equity and the civil rights for five racial or ethnic groups, we will want enrollments broken out by 1,160 categories, and their number can easily be multiplied again if we consider economic or educational disadvantagement, the special needs of language minorities, or service to students with one of eight handicapping conditions. Proceeding in this fashion, VEDS arrived at a reporting matrix amounting to about 10,000 cells of data (p. 9).

VEDS is an extreme case, but it illustrates the dangers of expecting too much of a data base. At best, tracking systems provide a limited, albeit invaluable set of indicators gauging student progress and outcomes. Table 1 provides an example, outlining the variables included in a student tracking model developed as part of a project begun in fall 1988 by AACJC to study the implementation of student tracking systems at colleges where none is in place. Similar in nature to the Texas LONESTAR system, the tracking model includes three sets of data for each student: (1) data on the attributes students bring with them to the colleges, including demographic characteristics, highest level of education attained, and academic ability as determined by basic skills entrance tests; (2) term-by-term indicators of student progress; and (3) follow-up information gathered after the student leaves the college. Attention to these variables provides valuable persistence and outcomes indicators. For example, degree completion rates that often appear shockingly low because of the small number of community college students who obtain certificates or associate degrees can be more accurately measured as the success rate of those students who intend to earn a degree or certificate in the first place. Similarly, the system also lays the groundwork for the calculation of

Table 1. Required Variables: AACJC Student Tracking Model

Student Attributes (collected at student entrance)	Student Progress (collected on a term-by-term basis)	Student Follow-Up (collected after the student leaves the college)

Name
ID number (social security no.)
Date of Birth
Ethnicity
Address
English as Native Language
Last school/college attended
highest level of schooling
  attained
Primary reason for attending
  this college at this time
Degree goal at this institution
Student major subject area
Reading, writing, math
  placement scores
	Information to be changed as necessary:
	  Name
	  Address
	  Degree goal at this college
	  Primary reason for attending
	  Declared major
	No. of college-level credits attempted
	No. of college-level credits completed
	No. of cumulative credits earned to date
	GPA for term
	Cumulative GPA
	No. of remedial credits attempted
	No. of remedial credits earned
		Was primary objective attained
		  in the student's opinion?
		Current employment status
		Relationship of job to college
		  studies
		Salary
		Hours per week employed
		Currently enrolled in college?
		  where
		major field of study
		credit hours lost in
		  transfer
		    GPA at new institution

meaningful transfer rates based on the transfer success of those students who enroll with the intention of preparing for transfer to four-year colleges or universities.

Numerous additional variables could be included in the model, such as socioeconomic status, disabilities, financial aid awarded, student satisfaction with the college experience, or employer satisfaction with the job performance of graduates. Indeed, student outcomes are potentially affected by any number of variables and can be assessed along numerous cognitive or affective lines. But the vast theoretical scope of outcomes assessment should not cloud the more practical task of building a data base. This task requires each college to select a limited but manageable set of indicators, realizing that many outcomes questions will remain unanswered. The resulting data base, though, will help assure that information on student attributes is collected accurately according to consistent definitions and related to student progress and outcomes. This will be a vast improvement over current ad hoc data collection practices and a necessary first step toward successful outcomes assessment.

Follow-Up Information

While data on student attributes and progress can often be culled from existing college records, information on students after they leave the college is more difficult to come by. The tracking model outlined in Table 1 assumes that information on the educational or vocational status of former students is somehow available, perhaps from follow-up surveys. In practice, however, accurate follow-up data are scarce. With signal exceptions, vocational follow-up surveys typically yield response rates of only 50 percent or less (Palmer, 1985). In addition, most community colleges do not have access to reliable data on the number of their students who transfer to four-year institutions. When such data are available, they are collected sporadically with inconsistent definitions of who a transfer student is (Cohen, 1988). Improved follow-up research is necessary if student tracking systems are to tie vocational and transfer outcomes to student educational objectives.

Part of the answer to this problem lies in limiting the number of students who are included in the follow-up portion of the tracking system. This focuses the survey research effort on smaller groups of respondents, thus increasing the probability of an acceptable response rate. Rather than surveying all students who have left the college, for example, follow-up analyses could focus only on those who have earned at least twenty-four units at the college and ignore students who have only taken two or three classes. Besides cutting down on research costs, the elimination of these students actually improves outcomes research, focusing it on those students for whom the college can legitimately take at least partial responsibility. It is doubtful that college effectiveness in transfer education and job training can be accurately assessed on the basis of follow-up information collected from those students who have had only a cursory exposure to the college's program of study.

Even if this step is taken, however, the success of follow-up tracking (as Stevenson, Walleri, and Japely note in Chapter Eight of this volume) will require a long-term resource commitment to survey research. The limited research capacity of most community colleges, evident in the dearth of student outcomes information currently available, makes it doubtful that most colleges can successfully tack on extensive follow-up surveys to existing data collection responsibilities. Demands from policymakers for information on what happens to students after they leave the college should be met with additional funding for research and an insistence that four-year colleges assist in tracking the educational experiences of community college transfer students.

Using Information

A final challenge lies in the degree to which data collected in student tracking systems are utilized to inform decisions affecting institutional planning and improvement. Harried institutional research officers often find that data collection and reporting chores leave little time for the analysis required to generate information. Accreditation guidelines tying outcomes assessment to evaluation of institutional effectiveness, however, will require that such analysis be given a higher priority.

If the tracking system is to assist in decision making and not be regarded as simply another data collection chore imposed from the outside, the entire college community, particularly faculty, should be involved in analyzing and interpreting the data. At a minimum this requires that reports generated by the system be distributed to faculty and not simply housed in the institutional research office. In addition, the reports should provide information that is meaningful to faculty. One way of doing this is to disaggregate outcomes data by program. "Those most familiar with student tracking systems indicate that unless student goals, performance, and follow-up information can be linked back to the major or program in which the student is or was enrolled, community college faculty and program staff cannot use the tracking information to improve their particular programs or address specific problems" (Coffey and Palmer, forthcoming, p. 35). It is for this reason that the tracking model outlined in Table 1 includes a variable for the student's self-reported major.

A danger, though, lies in the tendency of some to misinterpret the data generated by tracking systems as absolute measures of student outcomes. In fact, these data are indirect indicators that point to problem areas requiring further analysis. For example, the fact that job placement rates for vocational program A are higher than the job placement rates of vocational program B says little about the relative merits of the two programs. Further investigation is needed to determine why the rates differ and where program B can be improved, if necessary. As Ewell (1983) points out,

> The indicative quality of most student outcomes research is probably the aspect least well understood by its critics. . . . Most procedures for gathering data on student outcomes are indirect and will provide only partial information on a given outcome. Information gathered in this manner is ordinarily much more useful for the questions it raises than for the answers it provides [p. 62].

Summary

As a theoretical issue, student outcomes assessment has come to the fore, spurred by legislative interest and the demands of accrediting agencies. Many insist that the current interest in outcomes assessment, unlike educational issues that have come and gone in the past, is here to stay and not simply a flash in the pan. The final verdict, however, awaits further evidence that colleges can sustain the requisite data collection and research effort.

Student tracking systems are a necessary component of that effort. They hold great promise, especially in the potential to link student outcomes with student intentions. Only by making this link can community colleges generate accurate transfer rates, job placement rates, and other indicators of institutional effectiveness.

In practice, however, the implementation of tracking systems threatens to strain the research capacity of many colleges, requiring a shift in emphasis from the collection of cross-sectional data on enrollment and expenditures to the more difficult tasks of longitudinal data collection and analysis. While much attention has been paid to the need for outcomes-oriented data, relatively little attention has been paid to the factors affecting the ability of colleges to make this shift in research emphasis. Concern for the question "What do we want to know about students?" must be matched with equal concern for the question "How will we gather this information?" and "Who will provide the resources?"

References

Barnes, R. E. "Ten Years of Federal Statistics on Vocational Education." Paper presented at annual meeting of American Educational Research Association, New Orleans, La., April 23-27, 1984. 13 pp. (ED 245 108)

Coffey, J. C., and Palmer, J. *Implementing Student Tracking Systems at Community Colleges*. Washington, D.C.: American Association of Community and Junior Colleges, forthcoming.

Cohen, A. M. *Technical Report on the Urban Community College Transfer Opportunities Program*. Los Angeles: Center for the Study of Community Colleges, 1988. 13 pp. (ED 294 633)

Doan, H. M., and others. "Student Retention: A Longitudinal Study Tracking First-Time Students at an Urban Multi-Campus Community College." Paper presented at annual forum of Association for Institutional Research, Orlando, Fla., June 21–25, 1986. 17 pp. (ED 278 431)

Ewell, P. T. *Information on Student Outcomes: How to Get It and How to Use It*. Boulder, Colo.: National Center for Higher Education Management Systems, 1983. 89 pp. (ED 246 827)

Ewell, P. T. "Establishing a Computer-Based Assessment Program." In D. F. Halpern (ed.), *Student Outcomes Assessment: What Institutions Stand to Gain*. New Directions for Higher Education, no 59. San Francisco: Jossey-Bass, 1987.

Ewell, P. T., Parker, R., and Jones, D. P. *Establishing a Longitudinal Student Tracking System: An Implementation Handbook*. Boulder, Colo.: National Center for Higher Education Management Systems, 1988.

Lucas, J. A. *Longitudinal Study of Performance of Students Entering Harper College, 1974–1984*. Research Report Series Vol. 14, no. 6. Palatine, Ill.: William Rainey Harper College, Office of Planning and Research, 1986. 17 pp. (ED 264 931)

McConochie, D. *Four Years Later: Follow-Up of 1978 Entrants, Maryland Community Colleges, 1983*. Annapolis: Maryland State Board for Community Colleges, 1983. 37 pp. (ED 234 850)

National Council for Research and Planning. Unpublished tabulations. Bettendorf, Iowa, 1987.

Palmer, J. "Assessing the Employment Experiences of Community College Vocational Program Graduates: A Review of Institutional Follow-Up Studies." Graduate seminar paper, University of California at Los Angeles, 1985. 48 pp. (ED 258 665)

Jim Palmer is vice-president for communications services for the American Association of Community and Junior Colleges in Washington, D.C.

Index